Learn to use
two-hole beads

WITH 20 FABULOUS PROJECTS

Learn to use two-hole beads

WITH 20 FABULOUS PROJECTS

TERESA MORSE

A QUARTO BOOK

Learn to use two-hole beads with 20 fabulous projects

Kalmbach Books
21027 Crossroads Circle
Waukesha, Wisconsin 53186
www.Kalmbach.com/Books

First published in the United States in 2016 by Kalmbach Books

Published in 2016
19 18 17 16 15   1 2 3 4 5

ISBN: 978-1-62700-375-9
EISBN: 978-1-62700-376-6

Conceived, designed, and produced by
Quarto Publishing plc
The Old Brewery
6 Blundell Street
London N7 9BH
www.quartoknows.com

QUAR.DUOB

Editor & designer:
Michelle Pickering
Photographers:
Emma Robinson, Phil Wilkins
Illustrator: Teresa Morse
Design assistant: Martina Calvio
Art director: Caroline Guest
Creative director: Moira Clinch
Publisher: Paul Carslake

Color separation by PICA Digital Pte Ltd, Singapore
Printed by Hung Hing Off-Set Printing Co., Ltd, China

10 9 8 7 6 5 4 3 2 1

Library of Congress Control Number: 2015946884

Contents

Hello Beaders! 8

About This Book 9

Basics 10

Bead Box 12

Hardware 14

Toolkit 15

Basic Techniques 16

Beaded Findings 20

Designing with Color 24

Projects 28

One At a Time 30

Grow As You Go 46

Another Dimension 68

Dazzling with Crystals 90

Index and Credits 112

One at a time

Trinity Bracelet **31**

Mai Tile Bracelet Trio **34**

Summer Stars Necklace **42**

Grow as you go

New Leaf Necklace **47**

Demi Tuile Bracelet **50**

Daisy Chain Bracelet **52**

Mimosa Necklace **55**

Santi Drop Earrings **58**

Cascara Bangle **60**

Diamond Twist Bracelet **64**

Another dimension

Petits Secrets Bracelet **69**

Honesty Earrings **72**

Alicia Bracelet **74**

Wisteria Necklace **78**

Sparkling Swags Necklace **82**

Savannah Necklace **86**

Dazzling with crystals

Crystal Bloom Bracelet **91**

Triskele Pendant **94**

Corona Pendant **98**

Iona Pendant **102**

Cascade Necklace **106**

Cascade Ring **111**

Hello Beaders!

Two-hole beads have added a new dimension to bead weaving, slotting together in interesting ways to create exciting new shapes, textures, and styles. The beads come in lots of gorgeous colors and finishes, and are easily matched with seed beads, pearls, and crystals. Having two holes also makes them relatively quick to bead with, so you can have a brand new pair of earrings or a bracelet in just a few hours.

When I was a little girl, my mother had a beautiful beaded necklace; it was more than 100 years old at the time, and African, I believe. It was a carved ivory pansy on a chain of little blue daisies beaded with tiny blue, white, and yellow beads. It fascinated me. I would sneak into her jewelry box and fish it out to feel it, play with it, and wear it. Sadly, I broke it—the beads scattered and all that is left is the ivory pansy. I also owned a little Native American doll dressed in brown suede with tiny beads sewn on. She was my favorite, because of the beads.

As I grew older and began making jewelry, I experimented with lots of different methods. When I discovered beadweaving and bead embroidery, I was smitten. I spent a small fortune on beads while I learned everything I possibly could from books and

magazines, playing around with stitches and teaching myself how to do spirals, shaped beadwork, and leaves (my favorite thing).

As is my wont, I became bored with following everyone else's designs, and began creating my own. At the same time, SuperDuo and Twin beads had just come onto the market, and curiosity got the better of me. I found a video tutorial for a simple pendant, and using the new two-hole beads, I set about making it just to get the feel of them.

That was it! My creative instincts kicked in and a half-dozen designs were soon sketched, notes made, and pieces beaded. Now, I'm not one to keep things to myself. I like to share, so I acquired a few programs for my laptop and set about learning how to put together my designs into a workable form of instruction. I sent one of the designs as a kit to an experienced beader I know, who corrected a few mistakes and made some very useful suggestions, and there was my first beading tutorial. The rest is history.

Two-hole beads, like the SuperDuo and Twin beads you will be using to make the projects in this book, are not as challenging as you might think. Many existing beading techniques are used in a modified form to weave them together. Experienced beaders will recognize similarities to many standard beading stitches, particularly peyote stitch, netting, and fringing.

However, you certainly don't need to be an experienced beader to make any of the projects. Each project has detailed instructions, clear photographs of every stage, and diagrams for the more tricky parts where needed. You will find an eclectic range of styles and designs, along with different methods of putting them together. In the first section, we deal with single motifs, making one at a time and then joining them at the end to finish the design. Then in section two we move on to continuous weaving. Section three deals with texture and layers, and finally, the last section is dedicated to jewelry featuring sparkling crystal rivolis.

All you need to get started is good light, a needle and thread, and a pile of beads. All of the designs in this book are open to further interpretation. You can add embellishments of your own, change the colors around, and adapt the basic design to make your piece unique to you. Above all, have fun with your beading!

Teresa Morse

About This Book

Each project is self-contained and clearly set out with all the information you need to get started. See the design grow on the page, and watch your own creation grow alongside it. Here are some of the main features.

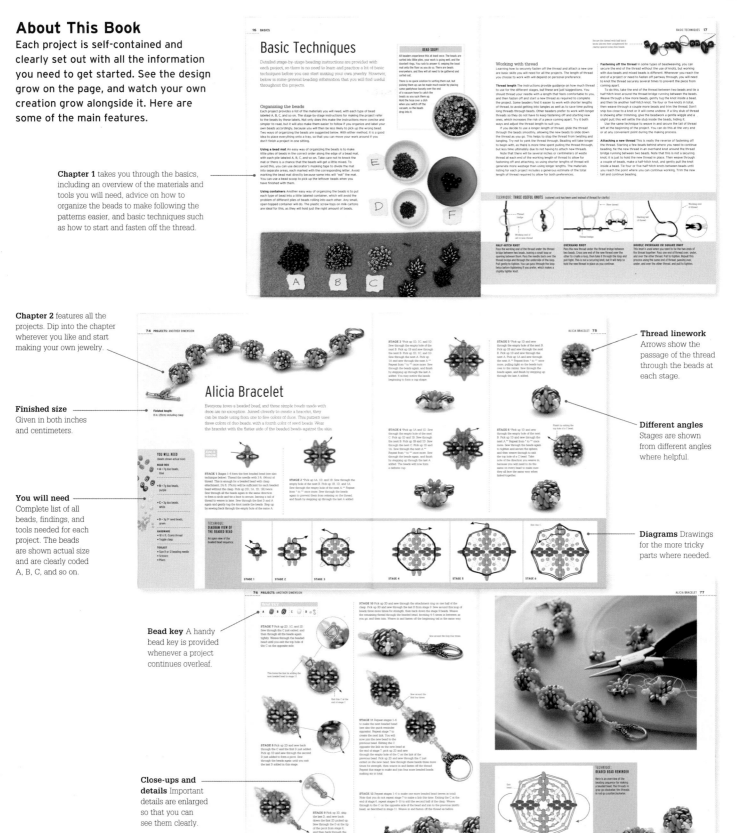

Chapter 1 takes you through the basics, including an overview of the materials and tools you will need, advice on how to organize the beads to make following the patterns easier, and basic techniques such as how to start and fasten off the thread.

Chapter 2 features all the projects. Dip into the chapter wherever you like and start making your own jewelry.

Finished size
Given in both inches and centimeters.

You will need
Complete list of all beads, findings, and tools needed for each project. The beads are shown actual size and are clearly coded A, B, C, and so on.

Bead key A handy bead key is provided whenever a project continues overleaf.

Close-ups and details Important details are enlarged so that you can see them clearly.

Thread linework
Arrows show the passage of the thread through the beads at each stage.

Different angles
Stages are shown from different angles where helpful.

Diagrams Drawings for the more tricky parts where needed.

Basics

All you really need to get started is a needle and thread and some beads, but as your collection of jewelry grows, so will your bead box and toolkit, which will gradually fill with all of the materials and tools you like best. This chapter outlines all of the essentials for working and finishing the projects, and at the end you will find guidance on choosing colors—remember, it's all about creating pieces to suit your own taste.

Bead Box

The projects in this book are designed to showcase two-hole beads and the beautiful jewelry designs that can be created from them. Each project also uses other types of beads, either to help weave and shape the two-hole beads or simply to embellish them.

Two-hole beads (1) There are new two-hole beads coming onto the market all the time. The projects in this book can be made using either SuperDuos, manufactured by Matubo in the Czech Republic, or Twin beads, made by Preciosa in the Czech Republic. The beads are referred to generically in the projects as "duo beads."

Both types of beads are oval, 5 x 2.5mm in size, and come in a variety of beautiful colors and finishes. The difference between them lies in the manufacturing process. Twins are made from extruded glass, meaning they are squeezed through tubes, rather like toothpaste, and then cut, drilled, and pressed while still hot and soft. This process does not produce perfectly uniform beads, making them less suitable for sculpted designs but perfect for freeform work. *Cull rates* (the number of beads that have to be discarded due to misshapes, or partials) is slightly higher for this reason, too.

SuperDuos are made from pressed glass, and have a little raised bump in the middle that allows them to slot together perfectly. These are preferable for sculpted and precision beadwork, but less suitable for freeform work.

There is marginal difference in the cost of the two brands, though it is good to remember that, while you will get approximately 15 beads per gram of SuperDuos, and roughly 20 beads per gram of Twins, you are likely to discard more Twin beads.

All the projects in this book have been made using SuperDuos. To achieve uniformity in a sculpted design like the Savannah Necklace (page 86), I recommend using SuperDuos rather than Twins, but for all other projects, either bead will give you excellent finished results. I recommend that you do not use both together.

Seed beads (2) All of the projects in this book use round seed beads, also known as rocailles. Japanese Miyuki or Toho seed beads are excellent for beadweaving because of their consistency, but there are many good European brands you can use, too—just be sure to use good-quality seed beads for even results. Seed beads come in several sizes, specified as the size number followed by º or /0 ("aught"). Sizes 15º, 11º, and 8º are used in this book. The bigger the number, the smaller the bead, because it once related to the number of beads per inch. Seed beads come in many finishes, including metallic, opaque, matte, transparent, frosted, and lined. They are made from glass, and will shatter to fine powder if you crush them with pliers (useful if you accidentally add an extra one, but be careful not to cut the thread).

COMPARING DUO BEADS

These triangle motifs for the Trinity Bracelet (page 31) are made with SuperDuos (near right) and Twin beads (far right), in similar colors. The SuperDuos nestle comfortably together due to the little bump in the middle, while the Twins don't quite do that, even though they sit together very well. In the finished bracelet, you would see little or no difference.

SuperDuos   Twin beads

Cylinder beads (3) These little glass beads are cylindrical in shape, uniform in size, and slot together beautifully to create shaped beadwork. Good-quality brands include Miyuki Delicas and Toho Treasures. They are readily available in most good bead suppliers. Size 11º are used in the projects.

Glass pearls (4) Round glass pearls are used in many of the projects. There are many good brands available, and all at a reasonable price. Be aware that some of the less expensive ones may not be perfectly round; there may be a dimple on each side where the hole is, making them slightly flattened. This may make it difficult to fit them into your beadweaving neatly. It is therefore worth spending just a little more on good brands, like Preciosa or Swarovski, as these are very round and the finish is less likely to peel or flake over time. The two sizes used in this book are 4mm and 6mm.

Faceted crystal beads (5) These lovely little fire-polished beads will add a bit of sparkle and embellishment to your work, with their faceted sides catching and reflecting light in all directions. Made from glass with machine-cut facets, they are glazed at extremely high temperatures to give them their gloss and shimmer. Round 4mm, 6mm, and 8mm crystals are used in the projects.

Crystal bicones (6) These gorgeous diamond-shaped beads reflect light, adding a twinkle to your beadwork. There are many brands available for all budgets, and many stand up very well to the best of them all, made by Swarovski, although nobody can imitate the perfect cut of a Swarovski Elements crystal bead. They come in a variety of sizes; 4mm bicones are used in this book.

Drop beads (7) These teardrop-shaped beads are designed to dangle. Crystal and pearl drops with a hole drilled vertically through the bead are used in the projects.

Rivolis (8) The cut of these crystals, and the fact they are foil-backed, gives them beautiful depth of color with a shimmering quality. Round in shape and pointed on both sides, rivolis don't have holes to thread them. Instead, you have to bead around them to create a bezel that holds them securely. They are made in several sizes, with 12mm and 14mm being used in this book.

Hardware

In addition to beads, the other materials you will require to make the projects include thread and findings. Findings include clasps, ear wires, jump rings, chains, and so on.

Thread (1) There are many kinds of thread available, and it is worth trying different types to see which you prefer. The projects in this book were made using braided fishing line, at 6 lb. test (breaking) strength. Although the colors are limited to crystal (clear) and smoke (gray), and occasionally green, the first two blend very well with most colors of beads, and the thread is fine enough to become almost invisible.

Nylon beading threads come in a whole spectrum of colors, and size D is the most common size used in beadwork. This will give a much softer feel to the work than using fishing line, but the thread will need to be conditioned with wax before use to avoid tearing, tangling, and fraying.

Clasps (2–4) There are numerous types of clasp to choose from. One of the most popular kinds is the toggle clasp (2), which has been used in many of the projects. Toggle clasps range from a basic plain loop and toggle, to fancy designs including square-shaped, heart-shaped, bejeweled, colored, and enameled. They work simply by inserting the toggle through the loop, making for an easy and secure fastening for necklaces and bracelets. Both parts come with an attachment ring, which you can join

to the beadwork with either a jump ring or by beading through it. There are also toggle clasps with two or more attachment rings for multi-strand necklaces and bracelets.

Magnetic clasps (3), which are perfect for bracelets if you struggle to fasten them, also come in various sizes, colors, finishes, and shapes. Most often you will find the round variety. These are like a ball cut in half, with a magnet in each half. Again, each half has an attachment ring to join to the jewelry.

Tube clasps (4) are perfect for multi-strand jewelry, having several attachment rings on each part. They are made of two tubes that fit one inside the other, sliding into place with a gentle click, and are often magnetic. They keep the multiple strands of a necklace separate, enabling the piece of jewelry to hang perfectly when worn.

Ear wires or hooks (5–6) There are many styles of earring findings. Most commonly used are the fish-hook or shepherd's hook style (5). Simple and inexpensive, these come in many different metals, from base copper plated with silver or gold, to sterling silver and surgical steel. Many come with tiny plastic pieces called *stoppers* or *keepers*, which can be used to prevent the hook from slipping out of the ear.

The kidney wire (6) is similar to the fish-hook, but has a little latch on the back to clip the end into for more security.

Lever-back ear hooks are ideal for slightly heavier earrings, and usually come with a little embellishment on the front, either some pre-set stones or just an additional fancy shape. They have a lever on the back that clicks into place, giving security.

Jump rings (7) These are little metal rings, usually cut at one point to enable you to open and close them. They can be used to attach findings to beaded jewelry or as temporary markers. Made of round wire, jump rings come in various sizes and thicknesses, and generally a 24-gauge ring suffices for most projects.

Pendant fittings (8–10) To finish a pendant, you will need something to hang it on. Chains (8) come in many sizes and styles. Some have a clasp already attached, or you can fit your own. For a softer look, try using ribbon or cord (9). Depending on the design, you may need a bail (10) to connect the pendant.

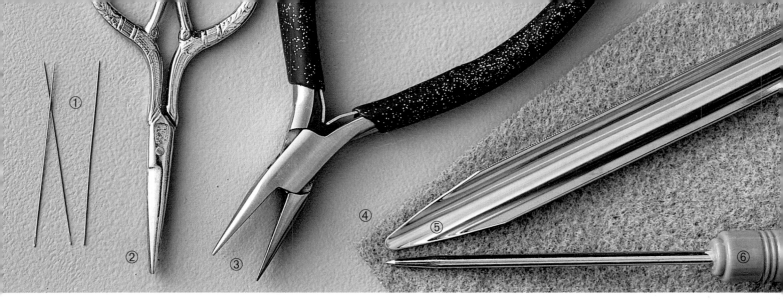

Toolkit

You will not get much beading done without the right tools. These are the essentials you will need to get started.

Needles (1) A size 11 or 12 beading needle is recommended for all the projects. These fine needles allow for many passes of the thread through the beads, but they can bend easily and sometimes break. Tulip, a Japanese brand of needle, is more expensive than some others, but is made of slightly springy steel and usually lasts much longer before you need to replace it (although all needles will eventually bend into an S shape with use).

There are other kinds of beading needles on the market, including really fine ones made of twisted wire, but these are a little too flexible for this kind of beading. There are also long-eye needles that have the eye along the entire length of the needle, making for easier threading, but I find that they can tear threads inside the eye as they get older.

Scissors (2) You will need small, sharp scissors for most projects, to trim the thread as closely as possible to the beads. If you are using braided fishing line as your threading material, set aside a pair of scissors solely for this purpose, as fishing line will dull the blades in time. Another option for trimming ends neatly is a thread zapper, a little tool that will melt a thread in place using a minute burner for precision. A gentle wiggle of the work will ensure that the closely snipped thread end will disappear inside the nearest bead.

Pliers (3) Both chain-nose and long-nose pliers are handy tools to use, for opening and closing the loops on ear wires, jump rings, and so on. Also, if you are struggling to get a needle through a bead that already has several threads running through it, you can use pliers to push the needle through until there is enough to grip with the pliers and pull through the other side. Be careful, though, that forcing a needle through does not break the bead.

Bead mat (4) Absolutely essential, a microfiber bead mat will not only keep your work in one place, and allow you to store your needles on it, but it will also stop beads from rolling and bouncing should you drop them. Bead mats last a long time, and are washable. You can also use velvet bead mats, which come in darker colors, too. You can cut down the mat to fit into a work tray, which can then be moved around safely and used for storing ongoing projects until finished.

Bead scoop (5) When a project is finished, you will need to clear away all those leftover beads and return them to their containers. This scoop is by far the best thing to have around. You can simply scoop them up and tip them into their pots or bags—far easier than picking up beads with your fingers.

Awl (6) Not only is this tool useful to have around when you find a blocked hole in a bead (and this often happens with duo beads), but it is also handy for untangling threads, unpicking work with several passes of thread through one bead, and separating threads without tearing or breaking them.

If you accidentally add an extra bead and you are too far along to unpick, you can also use the awl to break the bead without compromising the thread. Crushing with pliers does the same thing, but can cut the thread as the bead shatters. Pushing the tip of the awl up through the rogue bead and forcing the bead down will break it safely.

Basic Techniques

Detailed stage-by-stage beading instructions are provided with each project, so there is no need to learn and practice a lot of basic techniques before you can start making your own jewelry. However, below is some general beading information that you will find useful throughout the projects.

Organizing the beads

Each project provides a list of the materials you will need, with each type of bead labeled A, B, C, and so on. The stage-by-stage instructions for making the project refer to the beads by these labels. Not only does this make the instructions more concise and simpler to read, but it will also make them easier to follow if you organize and label your own beads accordingly, because you will then be less likely to pick up the wrong bead. Two ways of organizing the beads are suggested below. With either method, it is a good idea to place everything onto a tray, so that you can move your work around if you don't finish a project in one sitting.

Using a bead mat An easy way of organizing the beads is to make little piles of beads in the correct order along the edge of a bead mat, with each pile labeled A, B, C, and so on. Take care not to knock the mat or there is a chance that the beads will get a little mixed. To avoid this, you can use decorator's masking tape to divide the mat into separate areas, each marked with the corresponding letter. Avoid marking the bead mat directly because some inks will "eat" the mat. You can use a bead scoop to pick up the leftover beads when you have finished with them.

Using containers Another easy way of organizing the beads is to put each type of bead into a little labeled container, which will avoid the problem of different piles of beads rolling into each other. Any small, open-topped container will do. The plastic screw-tops on milk cartons are ideal for this, as they will hold just the right amount of beads.

BEAD SOUP!

All beaders experience this at least once. The beads are sorted into little piles, your work is going well, and the doorbell rings. You rush to answer it, swiping the bead mat onto the floor as you do so. There are beads everywhere, and they will all need to be gathered and sorted out.

There is no quick solution to sorting them out, but picking them up can be made much easier by placing some pantyhose loosely over the end of a vacuum hose to catch the beads as you suck them up. Hold the hose over a dish when you switch off the vacuum, so the beads drop into it.

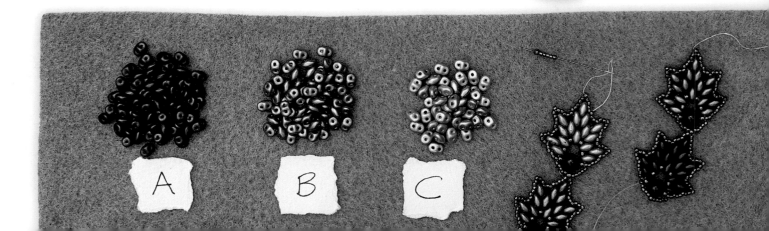

Secure the thread with half-hitch knots (shown here untightened for clarity) spaced every few beads.

Working with thread

Learning how to securely fasten off the thread and attach a new one are basic skills you will need for all the projects. The length of thread you choose to work with will depend on personal preference.

Thread length The instructions provide guidance on how much thread to use for the different stages, but these are just suggestions. You should thread your needle with a length that feels comfortable to you, and then fasten off and start a new thread as required to complete the project. Some beaders find it easier to work with shorter lengths of thread, to avoid getting into tangles as well as to save time pulling long threads through beads. Other beaders prefer to work with longer threads so they do not have to keep fastening off and starting new ones, which increases the risk of a piece coming apart. Try it both ways and adjust the thread length to suit you.

If you decide to use a longer length of thread, glide the thread through the beads smoothly, allowing the new beads to slide down the thread as you go. This helps to stop the thread from twisting and tangling. Try not to yank the thread through. Beading will take longer to begin with, as there is more time spent pulling the thread through, but less time ultimately due to not having to attach new threads.

Note that there will be several inches or centimeters of waste thread at each end of the working length of thread to allow for fastening off and attaching, so using shorter lengths of thread will generate more wastage than using longer lengths. The materials listing for each project includes a generous estimate of the total length of thread required to allow for both preferences.

Fastening off the thread In some types of beadweaving, you can secure the end of the thread without the use of knots, but working with duo beads and mixed beads is different. Whenever you reach the end of a project or need to fasten off partway through, you will need to knot the thread securely several times to prevent the piece from coming apart.

To do this, take the end of the thread between two beads and tie a half-hitch knot around the thread bridge running between the beads. Weave through a few more beads, gently tug the knot inside a bead, and then tie another half-hitch knot. Tie four or five knots in total, then weave through a couple more beads and trim the thread. Don't snip too close to a knot or it will come undone. If a tiny stub of thread is showing after trimming, give the beadwork a gentle wiggle and a slight pull; this will settle the stub inside the beads, hiding it.

Use the same technique to weave in and secure the tail of thread left at the beginning of the project. You can do this at the very end or at any convenient point during the making process.

Attaching a new thread This is really the reverse of fastening off the thread. Starting a few beads behind where you need to continue beading, tie the new thread in an overhand knot around the thread bridge running between two beads. Note that this is not a securing knot; it is just to hold the new thread in place. Then weave through a couple of beads, make a half-hitch knot, and gently pull the knot inside a bead. Tie four or five half-hitch knots between beads until you reach the point where you can continue working. Trim the new tail and continue beading.

TECHNIQUE: THREE USEFUL KNOTS (colored cord has been used instead of thread for clarity)

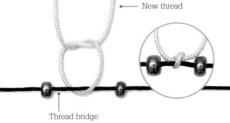

New thread

Thread bridge

Working end of old or new thread

Thread bridge

Starting tail of thread

Working end of thread

HALF-HITCH KNOT
Pass the working end of the thread under the thread bridge between two beads, leaving a small loop or opening between them. Pass the needle back over the thread bridge and through the underside of the loop. Pull gently to tighten. You can pass through the loop twice before tightening if you prefer, which makes a slightly tighter knot.

OVERHAND KNOT
Pass the new thread under the thread bridge between two beads. Cross one end of the new thread over the other to create a loop, then take it through the loop and pull tight. This is not a securing knot, but it will help to hold the new thread in place as you continue.

DOUBLE OVERHAND OR SQUARE KNOT
This knot is used when you need to tie the two ends of the thread together. Pass one end of thread over, under, and over the other thread. Pull to tighten. Repeat this process using the same end of thread, passing over, under, and over the other thread, and pull to tighten.

Gently push the tip of an awl into the bead hole to remove a blockage.

Starting to bead

Several methods are used in the projects to hold the first few beads in place while you get started.

Using a stop bead One method is to use a stop bead. This is a single bead, usually slightly larger than the project beads, that is positioned on the thread to stop the project beads from slipping off. Once the first few project beads are securely in place, you can remove the stop bead by sliding it over the end of the thread. As an alternative, you can simply wrap the tail end of the thread around a finger to stop the beads from falling off.

Starting with a circle of beads Many of the projects begin by sewing through a group of beads twice to form a circle. This secures the first few beads on the thread. Sometimes, especially with duo beads, it is necessary to knot the two ends of the thread together with a double overhand or square knot (see technique panel on page 17) to hold the circle of beads tightly in place while you continue beading. At other times, no knot is used. This may be to keep the beads relaxed and allow a little bit of movement during the next stage of beading, or because a knot would inhibit the passage of the thread through the beads at a later stage. Note that you can use a stop bead in these instances if you wish.

Dealing with blocked bead holes

The manufacturing processes involved in making two-hole beads—pressing, coating, and finishing—mean that you are likely to find a few blocked holes. It is usually caused by excess coating or a tiny piece of glass. If you find a blocked hole when using seed beads,

simply discard the bead. However, as there are fewer duo beads per gram than seed beads, it is not always better to discard them. Instead, use a bead awl or needle to gently push the blockage out of the hole. If it does not unblock easily or if the bead breaks, then discard it.

Always check two-hole beads for blocked holes before incorporating them into your beadwork, as there is nothing worse than having to unpick a whole section because a bead breaks while trying to unblock it. Take care to check with your needle, not with your eyes—you won't always see the blockage. You can check them as you go along by using the needle to pick up the bead through one hole. If the hole is clear, put the bead down and pick it up again through the other hole in order to check that one.

Stepping up

This simply means sewing through a specified bead in order to move the thread to a new position, ready to begin the next stage. Most of the stepping up in this book is done using the two holes of a duo bead. To step up through a duo bead, you will be passing the thread through one hole in one direction, and then passing the thread back through the second hole of the same bead in the opposite direction. Sometimes a few seed beads are added to hide the thread running between the two holes from view.

Note that if you are making a circular or tubular pattern, after stepping up you will be working in the opposite direction around the circle for the next stage. When working in rows, you will usually be working back across the row in the next stage. However, sometimes a pattern may require you to use a seed bead to allow you to turn and

---

TECHNIQUES: STARTING TO BEAD

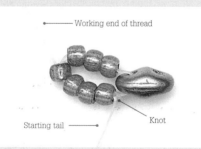

Working end of thread

Starting tail

Knot

STEPPING UP

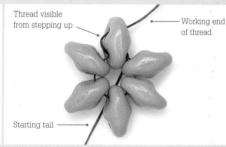

Thread visible from stepping up

Working end of thread

Starting tail

STOP BEAD
If using a one-hole bead as a stop bead, pass the thread through the bead twice in the same direction. Pull to tighten and slide the bead to where you want the work to begin. If using a duo bead, pass the thread through one hole and then back through the other hole. Pull the thread tight and slide the bead into the desired position.

CIRCLE OF BEADS
Pick up the beads indicated in the instructions. Sew through all the beads again in the same direction to form a circle, leaving a tail of thread to weave in later. If instructed to do so, tie the two ends of thread together with a knot to secure. As you continue beading, gently tug the knot inside the beads.

IN A CIRCLE
Take the needle through the first hole in the duo bead in one direction (here, counterclockwise), then carry the thread up to the second hole and take the needle through the same bead in the opposite direction (here, clockwise). You are now ready to work the next stage of beading (in this example, in a clockwise direction).

sew back through the same hole of the duo bead before stepping up through the other hole, so the thread continues in the same direction as before. "Turn" beads are often used for shaping the beadwork.

Attaching a clasp

All clasps have a small ring for attaching it to the piece of jewelry. The projects in this book use jump rings or a small loop of seed beads to attach the clasp, and full instructions are provided for each project.

Using a loop of beads Most of the projects use a loop of beads that can be swiveled around to ensure the clasp itself lies in the correct position. The thread is taken through the bead at the end of the piece of jewelry, then a new loop of beads is added going through the attachment ring on the clasp. The thread is taken back through the first bead of the new loop and then through the bead at the end of the piece of jewelry again. It is the two-directional weaving through the first bead of the loop—think of it as a pivot bead—that enables the bead loop to swivel if needed. Always sew around these beads several times for strength. Depending on the size of the bead holes, this is usually four times for 11º beads or three times for 15º beads.

Using jump rings You need two pairs of pliers for this, such as two pairs of long-nose or chain-nose pliers. Many beading toolkits come with a pair of long-nose pliers and a pair of round-nose pliers, and you can use these just as well. Open and close jump rings by twisting the two ends apart. Place the open jump ring through a loop of beads at the end of the jewelry and through the attachment ring on the clasp, and close again.

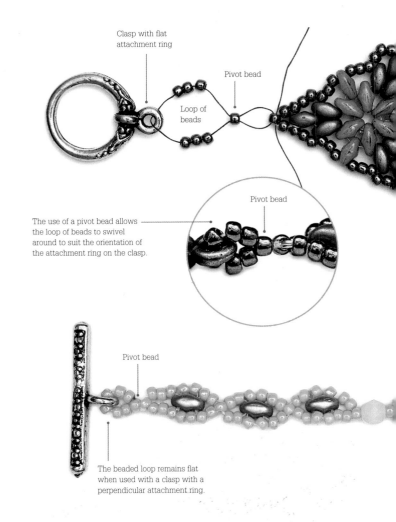

Clasp with flat attachment ring

Pivot bead

Loop of beads

Pivot bead

The use of a pivot bead allows the loop of beads to swivel around to suit the orientation of the attachment ring on the clasp.

Pivot bead

The beaded loop remains flat when used with a clasp with a perpendicular attachment ring.

ATTACHING A CLASP

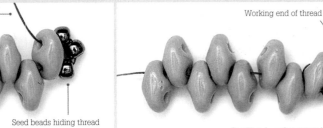

Working end of thread

Seed beads hiding thread from stepping up

Working end of thread

Seed bead used as a turn bead

Twist the other pliers toward you.

Twist one pair of pliers away from you.

AT THE END OF A ROW
Take the needle through to the last duo bead in the row. Pass the thread through the first hole in the duo bead, then carry the thread up to the second hole and take the needle through the same bead in the opposite direction. In this example, three seed beads have been added to cover the thread when stepping up.

USING A TURN BEAD
If you need to step up at the end of the row but continue working in the same direction, you can do so using a turn bead. Take the thread through the first hole of the last duo bead in the row. Pick up a seed bead, turn, and sew back through the hole just exited in the duo bead. Carry the thread up to the second hole and take the needle through the same duo bead.

OPENING AND CLOSING JUMP RINGS
Open and close jump rings by twisting them apart using two pairs of pliers. DO NOT pull the ends of the ring apart because this will put strain on the wire. Instead, twist one pair of pliers toward you, and the other away from you. Use the same twisting motion to close the jump ring again. You should feel the two ends grate together as you do this. Take care not to mark the jump ring with the pliers.

Beaded Findings

Ready-made clasps have been used throughout the book, and each pendant has instructions for making a simple beaded bail or hanging loop. However, sometimes you may want something a bit more special, so as a little bonus, here are an additional bail and toggle clasp that you can make yourself. Use beads left over from the main project to ensure a perfect match.

Large Beaded Bail

The instructions for two simple beaded bails are provided with the pendant projects on pages 97 and 105, but you might desire a slightly more chunky or robust bail, perhaps to fit around a spiral rope as shown below. This example has been made using beads to match the Iona Pendant (page 102). You can make the bail using the working thread from the pendant instead of fastening it off, or you can attach a new length of thread if required.

YOU WILL NEED
(beads shown actual size)

BEAD BOX
• **A** = 2g duo beads, turquoise

• **B** = 1g 11º seed beads, green

HARDWARE
• 2¹/₂ ft. (75cm) thread

TOOLKIT
• Size 11 or 12 beading needle
• Scissors

Finished size:
20mm wide x 18mm high

The size of the beaded bail can be adjusted to accommodate the thickness of the chain or cord you are using, such as this beaded spiral rope (you can find tutorials for making beaded chains online if you would like to make a similar one for your pendant).

Simple seed bead bail, page 97.

Simple duo bead bail, page 105.

See it
GROW

STAGE 1 Choose where you would like to attach the bail, and weave through the pendant to exit the uppermost bead. This may be a duo bead (as shown here) or a few seed beads, a pearl, or a crystal—it does not matter. Pick up 3B, 1A, and 3B. Sew back through the bead(s) at the top of the pendant. Sew through all the beads once more, and then through the first 3B and 1A again. Step up by sewing back through the empty hole of the same A.

This duo bead represents the uppermost bead of the pendant.

STAGE 2 B beads are now used as "turn" beads for sewing back and forth across the duo bead bail. Pick up 1A and 1B, turn, and sew back through the A just added and the A from stage 1. Pick up 1A and 1B, turn, and sew back through the A just added. Step up through the same A, making sure the beads are snug against the A from stage 1.

STAGE 3 Pick up 1A and 1B, turn, and sew back through the A just added and the next A. Pick up 1A and sew through the next A. Pick up 1A and 1B, turn, and sew back through the A just added. Step up through the same A.

STAGE 4 Pick up 1A and 1B, turn, and sew back through the A just added and the next A. [Pick up 1A and sew through the next A] twice. Pick up 1A and 1B, turn, and sew back through the A just added. Step up through the same A.

STAGE 5 Pick up 1A and 1B, turn, and sew back through the A just added and next A. [Pick up 1A and sew through the next A] three times. Pick up 1A and 1B, turn, and sew back through the A just added. Step up through the same A. If you need to, you can add more increase rows at this stage to make a bigger bail.

STAGE 6 You will now start the decrease rows. Pick up 1B, turn, and sew back through the A just exited. [Pick up 1A and sew through the next A] four times. Pick up 1B, turn, and sew back through 2A. Step up through the A just exited.

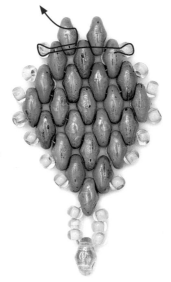

STAGE 7 Pick up 1B, turn, and sew back through the A just exited. [Pick up 1A and sew through the next A] three times. Pick up 1B, turn, and sew back through 2A. Step up through the A just exited.

STAGE 8 Pick up 1B, turn, and sew back through the A just exited. [Pick up 1A and sew through the next A] twice. Pick up 1B, turn, and sew back through 2A. Step up through the A just exited.

STAGE 9 Pick up 1B, turn, and sew back through the A just exited. Pick up 1A and sew through the next A. Pick up 1B, turn, and sew back through 2A. Step up through the A just exited.

STAGE 10 Pick up 3B, fold the bail over, and sew through the same bead(s) on the pendant as you did at the beginning. Pick up 3B and sew through the last A on the bail. Sew around these beads a few times to strengthen, then fasten off securely and trim.

Beaded Toggle Clasp

Making your own beaded clasp will give your project an extra special finish. This example has been made using beads to match the Cascade Necklace (page 106). The method of attaching the beaded clasp to the piece of jewelry will vary depending on the design. If there are one or two seed beads at the very end of the necklace strap or bracelet, simply join the clasp directly to these beads (as in stage 12). If there are no seed beads at the end (or you just think it would suit the design of the piece), you can create a small loop of seed beads to attach the clasp (as in stage 1).

Finished size: loop 24mm wide x 34mm long excluding link; toggle 34mm wide x 25mm long

YOU WILL NEED

(beads shown actual size)

BEAD BOX

* **A** = 1g duo beads, blue

* **B** = 1g 15º seed beads, dark green

* **C** = 2g 11º seed beads, green

* **D** = 1g 8º seed beads, green

* **E** = Two 4mm glass pearls, gold

HARDWARE

* 5 ft. (1.5m) thread

TOOLKIT

* Size 11 or 12 beading needle
* Scissors
* Stop bead

See it
GROW

STAGE 1 Use the working thread at the end of the bracelet or necklace strap, or attach a new 2 ft.(60cm) length and weave through to exit the last bead. If this last bead is a seed bead, you can skip to stage 2. Otherwise, make a small loop of seed beads by picking up 4C, 1D, and 4C. Sew through the bead(s) at the end of the strap to form a circle. Sew through all the beads once more, and then through the first 4C and 1D again.

This duo bead represents the last bead of the necklace or bracelet.

STAGE 2 Stages 2–4 form the loop of the clasp. Pick up 1C, [1D, 1A] seven times, [1D, 1C] twice, 1D, [1A, 1D] seven times, and 1C. Sew through the D from stage 1 (or the seed bead(s) at the end of the strap). Sew through all of the beads once more, and then through the first 1C, 1D, and 1A again. Step up by sewing back through the empty hole of the same A.

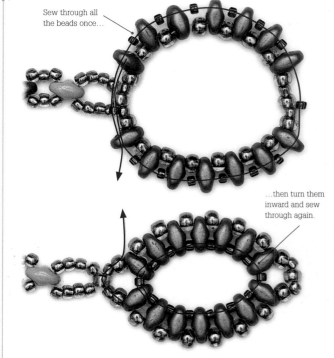

Sew through all the beads once…

…then turn them inward and sew through again.

STAGE 3 [Pick up 1B and sew through the empty hole of the next A] fourteen times. Sew through the first 1B and 1A again. Gently pull the thread to turn the A beads inward. Sew through all the beads once more and then step up through the A just exited. Sew through the 1D, 1C, 1D, 1C, and 1D around the end of the loop.

STAGE 4 [Pick up 2B, skip the next A, and sew through the next D] seven times. Sew through the next 1C, 1D, 1C, and 1D. [Pick up 2B, skip the next A, and sew through the next D] seven times. Weave in the remaining thread and fasten off securely.

STAGE 5 Stages 5–10 form the toggle, which is made using peyote stitch. Thread the needle with 3 ft. (90cm) of thread and add a stop bead, leaving a tail of thread to weave in later. Pick up 14C. These beads will form the first two rows of peyote stitch.

STAGE 6 Pick up 1C, skip the next C from stage 5, and sew through the next C. This forms peyote stitch. [Pick up 1C, skip the next C, and sew through the next C] six times. You now have three rows of peyote stitch.

STAGE 7 Repeat stage 6 another 11 times until there are 14 rows of peyote stitch in total.

Row 1
Row 2

Row 3

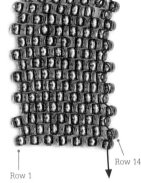

Row 1

Row 14

An open view of the thread path through the beads.

Tighten the thread to close the beads into a tube.

STAGE 8 Now join together the long ends of the peyote rectangle—rows 1 and 14—to form a small tube (see technique below).

STAGE 9 The ends of the tube look a little bare, so embellish them with more beads. Start by adding B beads around the first end of the tube (see technique below). Finish by exiting one of the top B beads just added.

Sew through these three beads three times to secure.

STAGE 10 Pick up 1E and sew through the top B on the opposite side of the tube. Sew back and forth twice more to secure.

STAGE 11 Weave through the beads to exit a C at the other end of the tube. Repeat stages 9–10 to embellish this end. Weave through to exit a C bead halfway along the tube, and then make a narrow strip of peyote stitch to form the post (see technique below).

STAGE 12 Attach the post of the toggle to the strap with a loop of seed beads (as in stage 1) or, as in this example, simply sew through the seed bead(s) at the very end of the strap. Sew through this joining group of beads a few times to secure, and then weave in and fasten off the thread.

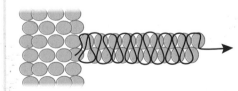

Adjust your joining method to suit the style of the piece of jewelry you are attaching the clasp to.

TECHNIQUE: MAKING THE TOGGLE

JOINING THE TUBE (STAGE 8)
Take the needle across the rectangle and sew through the first bead on row 1. Then sew through the second bead on row 14, the second bead on row 1, the third bead on row 14, and so on until you reach the end. Pull tight to join the beads together. Sew around the last two beads a couple of times to secure.

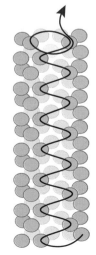

EMBELLISHING THE ENDS (STAGE 9)
Working across the C beads at the end of the tube, pick up 3B and sew down through the next C and up through the following C. *Pick up 2B and sew down through the third B in the previous group of 3B, and the C below. Sew up through the next 1C and 1B.** Pick up 2B and sew down through the next C and up through the following C.*** Repeat from * to *** once more, and then from * to ** once again.

MAKING THE POST (STAGE 11)
Exit a C halfway along the tube and pick up 2C. Sew back up through the C on the tube and the first C just added. *Pick up 1C and sew down through the C below. Pick up 1C and sew up through the C above.** Repeat from * to ** for the length required—17C will make a post of about ¾ in. (2cm).

Designing with Color

Many people like to use the same color scheme as the one shown in the project, because that is what attracted them to it. That is fine, but what if you want to use other colors? How do you decide which colors to use? This is the fun part.

Cascara Bangle (page 60) in complementary pink and green, with neutral gold.

Color theory

You can learn how to use color to great effect by exploring the basic principles of color theory. Designers in many fields use the color wheel to help them choose color schemes.

The color wheel This shows the relationship between different colors and how they work together. The color wheel is made of three primary colors—red, yellow, and blue. These are mixed in pairs to create the secondary colors that sit between them on the wheel—for example, the secondary color orange is a mixture of red and yellow. These in turn are mixed with their neighboring colors on the wheel to create the tertiary colors—red-orange, yellow-orange, and so on. Lighter tints (or pastels) can be created by adding white to each color; darker shades can be created by adding black to each color.

Complementary colors Colors that are opposite each other on the color wheel, such as red and green, are known as complementary (or contrasting) colors. Complementary colors create vibrant color schemes with the greatest amount of contrast. Complementary colors may clash with each other when used at full strength, so try using softened tints and shades for a rich, rather than clashing, result. Often, the best results are achieved by using different proportions of the colors, such as using 80 percent of the main color and 20 percent of a complementary color.

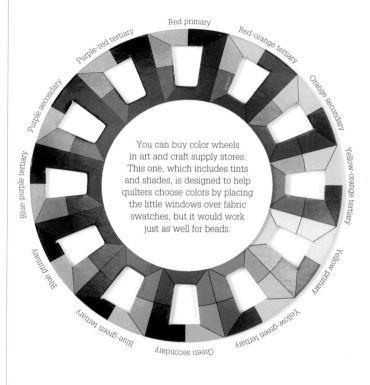

You can buy color wheels in art and craft supply stores. This one, which includes tints and shades, is designed to help quilters choose colors by placing the little windows over fabric swatches, but it would work just as well for beads.

Red primary · Red-orange tertiary · Orange secondary · Yellow-orange tertiary · Yellow primary · Yellow-green tertiary · Green secondary · Blue-green tertiary · Blue primary · Blue-purple tertiary · Purple secondary · Purple-red tertiary

Triskele Pendant (page 94) in two harmonious color schemes, one with neutral cream added.

Harmonious colors Colors that are next to each other on the color wheel, such as blue-purple, blue, and blue-green, are known as harmonious (or analogous) colors. Harmony is achieved because all the colors are quite similar. These are easy schemes to put together, allowing variety in color but not risking any jarring contrasts. Adding a small amount of a complementary color to a harmonious scheme will provide a bit of sparkle.

Neutral colors Neutral colors, such as white, black, cream, brown, and gray, do not appear as pure colors on the color wheel. They are made by mixing pure colors together. For example, mixing the three primaries together gives black. Mixing complementary colors together produces a range of grays and browns. Neutrals, therefore, work well with all the colors on the color wheel and can be used to great effect in beadwork, especially in backgrounds and to set off other colors.

Mimosa Necklace (page 55) worked in complementary red and green, with neutral black and bronze. Note how you can achieve very different results from the same colors simply by varying how you use the colors in the pattern.

PLAYING WITH COLOR

If you have a natural eye for color, and most beaders do, you can just lay out your newest main beads, and match other beads in your stash to it. Sometimes the beads "speak" to you by themselves, and look so natural against one another. Beads usually come in clear plastic bags or tubes, so it is easy to move them around and try different combinations laid together while you choose your palette.

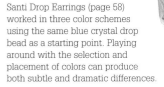

Santi Drop Earrings (page 58) worked in three color schemes using the same blue crystal drop bead as a starting point. Playing around with the selection and placement of colors can produce both subtle and dramatic differences.

TINTS AND SHADES

The intensity of a color scheme can be decreased by using color tints or shades. Adding white to a color produces a tint (or pastel color)—pale pink is a tint of red, for instance. Adding black to a color produces a shade—for example, burgundy is a shade of red. All of the different types of color schemes can be made using tints or shades to produce a more muted piece of jewelry.

New Leaf Necklace (page 47) worked in pastel pinks for a springtime color scheme, and deep red and burgundy with neutral gold and copper for a richer, autumnal look.

TONAL VALUE

Tonal value refers to whether a color is naturally light or dark. Lemon yellow has a very light tonal value, appearing almost white, while indigo has the darkest tonal value, appearing almost black. It is sometimes difficult to judge tonal values. The eye looks at the color first, and does not immediately consider the tonal value.

One way to comprehend this is to imagine taking a black-and-white photograph of the colors. Which beads would be the palest gray, and which the darkest gray? You can check the tonal value of beads or small samples of beadwork by taking a black-and-white photograph, or use a photo-editing program to change photographs to grayscale.

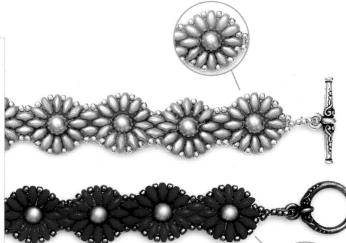

The color schemes used to make each of these Daisy Chain Bracelets (page 52) have little tonal contrast, as can be seen in the black-and-white (grayscale) details. The pattern of the top bracelet is more pronounced because of the greater color contrast of blue and pink, as opposed to red and pink.

The diamond pattern stands out well on both of these Diamond Twist Bracelets (page 64), but this is achieved in different ways. The top bracelet uses color contrast, while the bottom example uses tonal contrast.

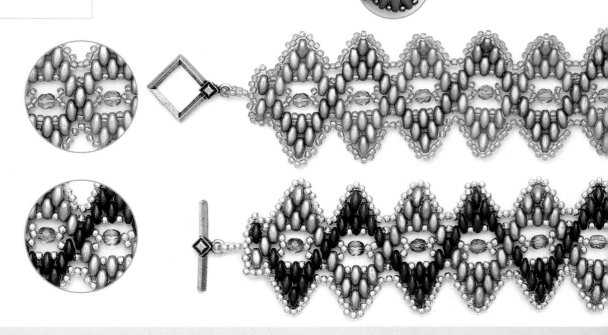

COLOR CASE STUDY:
SAVANNAH NECKLACE (PAGE 86)

Color can dramatically change the way a piece looks and feels. Five versions of the Savannah Necklace are shown here. The main project is made using a harmonious English rose palette, but the addition of complementary green to the pink palette creates a much more vibrant color scheme. The next three samples are made in colors influenced by Asian cultures, Native American traditions, and the Masai tribes of Africa. The latter two necklaces also feature pattern changes on the central diamond section. Each looks like a completely different piece, and has picked up the general "feel" of the culture that influenced it.

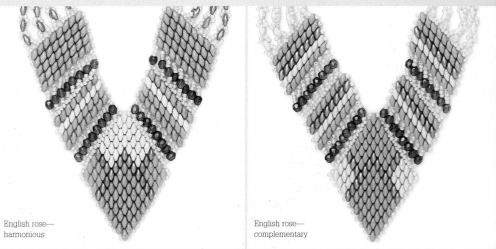

English rose—harmonious

English rose—complementary

Three examples of color palettes made using photographs of flowers as inspiration. If you don't have a photo-editing program, you can use paint or colored pencils to make a palette, or simply lay out your beads and select the nearest colors to the different parts of the photograph. Whatever method you use, the important thing is simply to create a palette that pleases you.

Color inspiration

Learning about color theory and how colors work together is all very well, but what if you get stuck when trying to choose colors for your projects? If this happens, simply look around you and find what is pleasing to your eye. For example, take a look online, especially at jewelry sites, and see which pieces pop out for you. You can then emulate those colors in your new piece.

Creating a color palette from nature Go for a walk and take some examples from nature. Take photographs of flowers and plants that you like, and use them in your beading. For example, the colors of spring forget-me-nots are so pleasing to the eye that they are clearly a perfect palette of colors that you can use in your beadwork.

If you have a photo-editing program (or a paint or draw program) on your computer, you can color-pick the main colors from the photograph and separate these into little squares or rectangles. This is your palette. You can tweak this palette a little, lighten some colors, and darken others. Limiting the palette to a maximum of six main colors, which can include various nuances, will give you a good selection to blend into your project. You can match your beads as closely as you can to these colors.

Cultural and artistic traditions You can use other things for inspiration in the same way as nature. A ceramic tile, especially those from other countries and tribal traditions, can inspire the perfect palette—for example, Native American turquoise, white, and fire colors (reds, yellows, oranges); African blue, red, green, yellow, and black; Asian gold, ruby, emerald, sapphire, and magenta. As with creating a palette from nature, simply find a picture, separate the colors to form a palette, and base your project on those.

Tip Good lighting
Good lighting is essential for beadwork. Poor light will mean eyestrain and mistakes. If you are lucky enough to have a big window to sit by as you bead, then do so. Invest in a good daylight lamp for the times when natural daylight is not available or bright enough. Make that investment—it is cheaper than spectacles. Try not to bead under halogen energy-saving lights. The orange tone really does interfere with color perception, and you risk making mistakes.

Asian

Native American

African/Masai

Projects

This chapter features more than 20 fabulous projects, with stage-by-stage instructions and photographs to explain in detail how to make each piece. The chapter is divided into four sections, with the projects grouped according to the method of construction, design features, or materials. So take your pick and explore the many ways in which duo beads can be used to create a world of color, shape, and texture.

One at a time

This section features a collection of beautiful jewelry made from individual beaded motifs that are made one at a time and then joined together at the end to complete the piece. The projects demonstrate how to make differently shaped motifs, and how to use beads to embellish and link them in simple yet creative ways.

Trinity Bracelet

This fabulous bracelet is made from duo bead triangles joined together with pairs of crystal beads to add some sparkle and fun. Each triangle is made one at a time and then linked together at the end.

See it GROW

STAGE 1 Stages 1–4 form the triangle unit. Thread the needle with 2 ft. (60cm) of thread and pick up 6A. Sew through all the beads again in the same direction to form a circle and tie a knot to secure, leaving a tail of thread to weave in later. Sew through the first 2A again and gently tug the knot inside the beads. Step up by sewing back through the empty hole of the A just exited.

STAGE 2 *Pick up 2B and sew through the empty hole of the next A. Pick up 1A and sew through the next A.** Repeat from * to ** twice more. Sew through the first B added and then step up through the same B.

STAGE 3 *Pick up 3C and sew through the empty hole of the next A. Pick up 3C and sew through the next B. Pick up 1B and sew through the next B.** Repeat from * to ** twice more. Sew through the first 3C, 1A, and 3C again.

Finished length:
7½ in. (19cm) including clasp

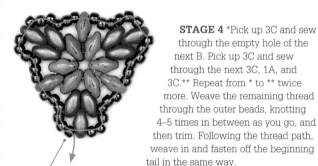

Exit this C when making the final (seventh) motif.

STAGE 4 *Pick up 3C and sew through the empty hole of the next B. Pick up 3C and sew through the next 3C, 1A, and 3C.** Repeat from * to ** twice more. Weave the remaining thread through the outer beads, knotting 4–5 times in between as you go, and then trim. Following the thread path, weave in and fasten off the beginning tail in the same way.

STAGE 5 Repeat stages 1– 4 to make seven triangles in total. For the last triangle, use 5 ft. (1.5m) of thread and do not fasten off. Instead, weave through to exit the C bead indicated above. You will use the extra thread to join the triangles together.

YOU WILL NEED (beads shown actual size)

BEAD BOX
- **A** = 5g duo beads, turquoise
- **B** = 5g duo beads, pink
- **C** = 4g 11° seed beads, bronze
- **D** = Twelve 4mm faceted crystal beads, red

HARDWARE
- 17 ft. (5.2m) thread
- Toggle clasp

TOOLKIT
- Size 11 or 12 beading needle
- Scissors

Bead KEY

A	B	C	D

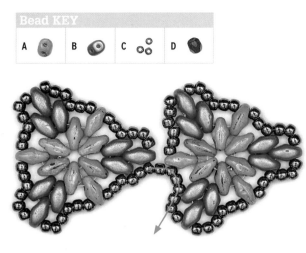

STAGE 6 You will start by joining the triangles along the lower edge. Pick up 1C and sew down through 5C below the A on the side of the second triangle.

STAGE 9 Pick up 3C, skip the B at the corner, and sew through the next 6C, 1A, and 6C along the side until you reach the B at the point of the second triangle.

STAGE 10 Repeat stages 6–9 until you have joined all of the triangles along the lower edge.

STAGE 7 Pick up 4C and sew up through 3C toward the point of the first triangle. Sew through the C added in stage 6 and 2C of the second triangle again.

STAGE 11 Pick up 3C and sew back through the B at the tip of the last triangle. Sew through the first 2C again.

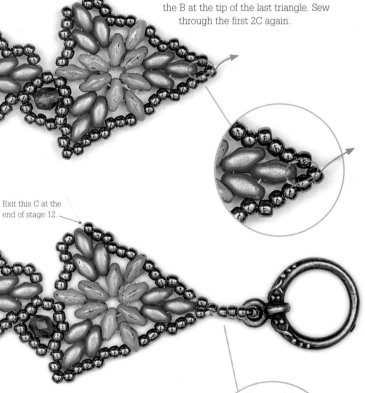

STAGE 8 Pick up 1D and sew up through 2C toward the point of the first triangle, the C added in stage 6, and the outer C beads of the second triangle to reach the B at the lower corner.

Exit this C at the end of stage 12.

STAGE 12 Pick up 4C and sew through the attachment ring on one half of the clasp. Pick up 3C and sew down through the first of the 4C and then through the middle C from stage 11. Sew around this loop of beads three more times for strength. Weave through the outer beads of the triangle until you exit the C before the B at the top corner.

Sew around the loop four times.

STAGE 13 You will now join the triangles along the upper edge. Pick up 3C and sew down through the next 6C on the side of this triangle. Pick up 1C and sew up through 3C on the next triangle.

STAGE 14 Pick up 4C and sew down through 5C toward the A on the last triangle. Sew through the 1C added in stage 13 and 2C on the next triangle.

STAGE 15 Pick up 1D and sew down through 2C toward the A on the last triangle. Sew through the 1C added in stage 13, then continue through the outer beads of the next triangle until you exit the C at the top corner (like at the end of stage 12).

Exit this C at the end of stage 16.

STAGE 16 Repeat stages 13–15 along the upper edge until you reach the other end, exiting the C indicated below on the final triangle.

STAGE 17 Repeat stages 11–12 to add the second half of the clasp, placing the stage 11 loop of 3C over the A. Weave in and fasten off the thread.

YOU WILL NEED

Refer to the instructions for
the bracelet you are making.

- **1** = Beach Mai Bracelet,
  pages 36-37
- **2** = Tic Tac Mai Bracelet,
  pages 38-39
- **3** = Daisy Mai Bracelet,
  pages 40-41

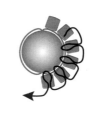
①

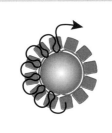
②

③

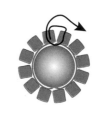

Mai Tile Bracelet Trio

Using the same basic Mai Tile unit, oriented as a square or a diamond, you can
make three very different bracelets. The instructions for making a single tile
are given first, followed by how to join them together to make each bracelet.
Be sure to use a perfectly round bead at the center. Some beads have a slight
dip where the hole goes through, which may cause the tile to curl.

Finished size of tile:
1 in. (2.5cm) square

TECHNIQUE: BEADING AROUND THE PEARL (STAGE 1)

STEP 1
Pick up 1E and sew through it four
times in the same direction to form
four loops of thread around the
outside. Place two loops on each
side of the E.

STEP 2
Pick up 2C. Take the needle under
the two threads on one side of
the E, then pass the needle up
through the second C.

STEP 3
*Pick up 1C. Take the needle
under the two threads and back
up through the C.** Repeat from
* to ** three more times so there
are 6C around this side of the E.

STEP 4
Add 6C around the second side
of the E in the same way. Exit
the last C added, ready to
anchor the beads together.

STEP 5
Take the needle down through the
first C added in step 2, then back
up through the last C. Pull the
thread gently to tighten, and
carefully straighten the beads.

Mai Tile

This sample uses the bead colors of the Beach Mai Bracelet, but the instructions are the same for all three bracelets.

STAGE 1 Thread the needle with 3 ft. (90cm) of thread and add a stop bead, leaving a tail of thread to weave in later. Pick up 1E and bead 12C around it (see technique opposite).

STAGE 2 Bead 24D around the C beads (see technique below).

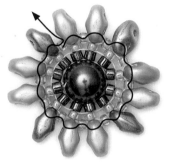

STAGE 3 *[Pick up 1A, skip the next D, and sew through the next D] twice. Pick up 1B, skip the next D, and sew through the next D.** Repeat from * to ** three more times.

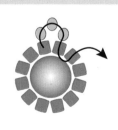

STAGE 4 *Pick up 3D and sew through the empty hole of the next A. Pick up 1A and sew through the next A. Pick up 3D and sew through the next D, B, and D.** Repeat from * to ** three more times. Sew through the first 3D added in this stage.

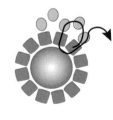

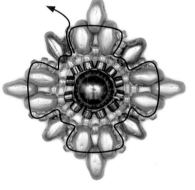

STAGE 5 *Pick up 3D and sew through the empty hole of the A from stage 4. Pick up 3D and sew through the next 2D from stage 4. Pick up 1D and sew through the empty hole of the next B. Pick up 1D and sew up through the next 2D from stage 4.** Repeat from * to ** three more times. Sew through the first 3D added in this stage.

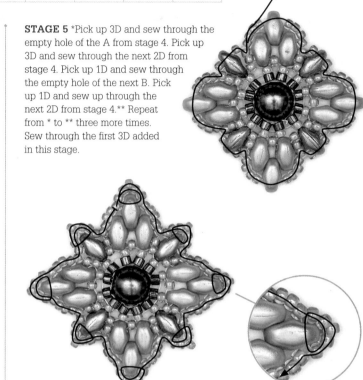

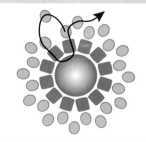

STAGE 6 *Pick up 4D and sew back through the duo bead and the first 2D just added. Pick up 1D and sew through the next 2D just added, forming a neat picot. Sew through the next 6D around the edge of the tile.** Repeat from * to ** seven more times. Weave the remaining thread through the beads, knotting 4–5 times in between as you go, but do not place any knots between the outer D beads because this will inhibit any passes of the thread when joining tiles together. Trim the thread, then fasten off the beginning tail in the same way.

TECHNIQUE: BEADING AROUND THE PEARL (STAGE 2)

STEP 1
Pick up 3D. Sew down through the next C and up through the following C.

STEP 2
*Pick up 2D. Sew down through the nearest D from the previous step and the C below it. Sew up through the next C and the first D just added.

STEP 3
Pick up 2D. Sew down through the next C and up through the following C.** Repeat from * to ** four more times. Sew up through the first D added in step 1.

STEP 4
Pick up 1D. Sew down through the last D added and the C below it. Sew up through the next C and 2D.

Beach Mai Bracelet

In this first of the three Mai Tile bracelets, the tiles are joined side by side with pearls in between to create a flattering summer bracelet.

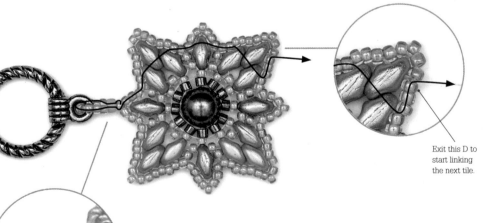

Finished length:
7½ in. (19cm) including clasp

YOU WILL NEED
(beads shown actual size)

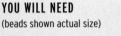

BEAD BOX
- A = 5g duo beads, blue
- B = 2g duo beads, gold
- C = 1g 11º cylinder beads, bronze
- D = 4g 15º seed beads, aqua
- E = Six 6mm glass pearls, bronze
- F = Two 11º seed beads, aqua
- G = Ten 4mm glass pearls, bronze

HARDWARE
- 21 ft. (6.4m) thread
- Toggle clasp

TOOLKIT
- Size 11 or 12 beading needle
- Scissors
- Stop bead

See it GROW

STAGES 1–6 Make six Mai Tiles (see page 35) and place five of them to one side. Thread the needle with 3 ft. (90cm) of thread. Attach the thread securely to one tile and weave through the beads to exit the D at the tip of the picot along one side, ready to attach the first half of the clasp.

Exit this D on the first tile to attach the clasp.

Exit this D to start linking the next tile.

Sew around the loop three times.

STAGE 7 Pick up 1F and 4D. Sew through the attachment ring on one half of the clasp. Pick up 4D and sew down through the F and then through the D at the tip of the picot. Sew around this loop of beads twice more for strength. Following the thread path, weave through the tile until you exit the D below the picot beads at the top right corner.

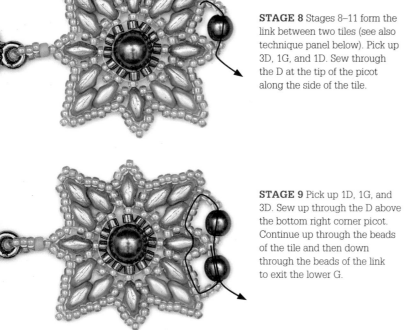

STAGE 8 Stages 8–11 form the link between two tiles (see also technique panel below). Pick up 3D, 1G, and 1D. Sew through the D at the tip of the picot along the side of the tile.

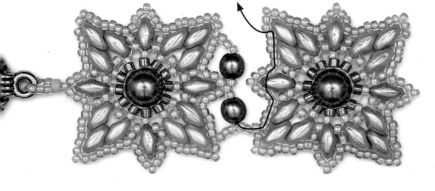

STAGE 9 Pick up 1D, 1G, and 3D. Sew up through the D above the bottom right corner picot. Continue up through the beads of the tile and then down through the beads of the link to exit the lower G.

STAGE 11 Pick up 3D and sew down through the next G and D of the link. Sew down through the D at the tip of the picot on the side of the second tile, then up through the next D of the link and the D at the tip of the picot on the first tile. Sew up through the next D of the link, down through the D at the tip of the picot of the second tile, and down through the next D and G of the link. Sew down through the first 3D added in stage 10, then weave through the beads of the second tile to exit the D as shown in stage 7.

STAGE 12 Repeat stages 8–11 until all six motifs are joined. On the last motif, continue weaving through the beads until you exit the D at the tip of the picot along the far side.

Exit this D on the final tile to attach the clasp.

STAGE 10 Pick up 3D and sew up through the D above the bottom left corner picot of the second tile. Sew up through the beads of that tile until you exit the D below the top left corner picot.

STAGE 13 Attach the second half of the clasp in the same way as before (stage 7). Weave in and fasten off the remaining thread.

TECHNIQUE: DIAGRAM VIEW OF LINKING THE TILES

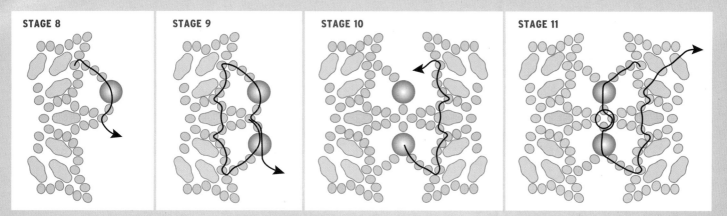

STAGE 8 | STAGE 9 | STAGE 10 | STAGE 11

Tic Tac Mai Bracelet

This bracelet plays with the colors and angles of the tiles. Three tiles use blue duo beads as the main color (A) and coral as the accent color (B); the colors are reversed in the remaining two tiles. The tiles are all joined with glass pearls, but at different angles to create alternating squares and diamonds.

See it GROW

STAGES 1–6 Make five Mai Tiles (see page 35), using blue duo beads as the main color for three of them and coral as the main color for the remaining two. The blue tiles will be used as squares, and the coral tiles as diamonds. Thread the needle with 4 ft. (1.2m) of thread and attach it securely to a blue square tile. Weave through the beads to exit the D at the tip of a picot along the side, ready to attach the first half of the clasp.

Make two coral diamond tiles.

Exit this D on the first tile to attach the clasp.

Make three blue square tiles.

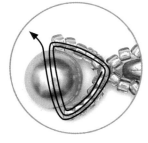

STAGE 7 Pick up 5D, 1E, and 5D. Sew back through the D at the tip of the picot. Sew through all the beads once more, then through the first 5D and E again.

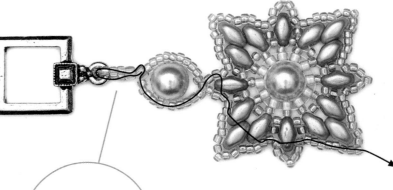

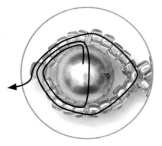

STAGE 8 Pick up 5D, 1F, and 5D. Sew through the E and then through all of the seed beads surrounding the E to join them neatly. Finish by exiting the F.

Sew around the loop three times.

STAGE 9 Pick up 1F and 4D. Sew through the attachment ring on one half of the clasp. Pick up 4D and sew down through the F just added and then through the F from stage 8. Sew around this loop of beads twice more for strength. Following the thread path, weave through the beads until you exit the D at the tip of the picot at the bottom right corner of the tile.

YOU WILL NEED (beads shown actual size)

BEAD BOX
- **A** = 4g duo beads, blue

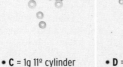

- **B** = 3g duo beads, coral

- **C** = 1g 11º cylinder beads, gold

- **D** = 3g 15º seed beads, gold

- **E** = Fifteen 6mm glass pearls, gold

- **F** = Four 11º seed beads, gold

HARDWARE
- 19 ft. (5.8m) thread
- Toggle clasp

TOOLKIT
- Size 11 or 12 beading needle
- Scissors
- Stop bead

STAGE 10 You will now join the tiles along the lower edge. Pick up 2D, 1E, and 2D. Sew through the D at the tip of the middle picot along the side of a diamond tile. Weave through the beads until you exit the D at the tip of the middle picot on the next lower side of the diamond tile. You can place a knot between beads to hold everything in place if you wish.

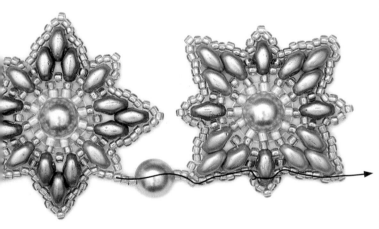

STAGE 11 Pick up 2D, 1E, and 2D. Sew through the D at the tip of the bottom left corner picot of the next square tile. Weave through the beads until you exit the D at the tip of the bottom right corner.

STAGE 12 Repeat stages 10–11 once more with the remaining tiles. Weave through the last square tile until you exit the D at the tip of the middle picot along the far side.

STAGE 13 Repeat stages 7–9 to attach the other half of the clasp, but finish by exiting the D at the tip of the picot at the top left corner of the tile.

Exit this D on the final tile to attach the clasp.

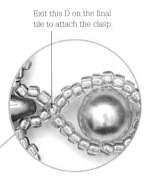

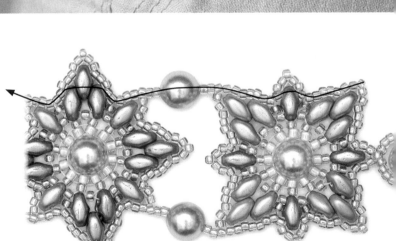

Finished length:
7 in. (18cm) including clasp

STAGE 14 Now join the tiles along the upper edge to match the lower edge (stages 10–11). Weave in and fasten off the remaining thread.

Daisy Mai Bracelet

Here, the Mai Tiles are joined using a little daisy flower as a link to make a delicate, elegant bracelet. You can use a single length of thread from end to end, but take care not to pull too tight or the tiles will curl.

STAGES 1–6 Make three Mai Tiles (see page 35) and put them to one side.

STAGE 7 Stages 7–10 form the first daisy. Thread the needle with 4 ft. (1.2m) of thread. Pick up [1F, 1B] ten times. Sew through all the beads again to form a circle, leaving a tail of thread to weave in later. Sew through the first F and B again, and then step up by sewing back through the empty hole of the same B.

The duo beads will turn inward as you tighten the thread.

STAGE 8 Loosely sew through all of the empty holes in the B beads. Tighten the thread, gently teasing the beads inward as you do so.

YOU WILL NEED
(beads shown actual size)

BEAD BOX
- **A** = 3g duo beads, pink
- **B** = 4g duo beads, gold
- **C** = 1g 11º cylinder beads, peach
- **D** = 3g 15º seed beads, peach
- **E** = Three 6mm glass pearls, peach
- **F** = 1g 11º seed beads, peach
- **G** = Four 4mm glass pearls, peach

HARDWARE
- 13 ft. (4m) thread
- Toggle clasp

TOOLKIT
- Size 11 or 12 beading needle
- Scissors
- Stop bead

STAGE 9 Pick up 1G and sew through the B opposite the B just exited. Sew back through the G and the first B, then pull tight. Sew through the G and the opposite B again, and step up through the same B. Sew through the next F.

STAGE 10 *Pick up 3D, skip the B, and sew through the next F.** Repeat from * to ** eight more times.

STAGE 11 Pick up 1D and sew through the D at the tip of the picot along the side of one of the tiles. Pick up 1D and sew through the B in the daisy to link the daisy and tile together. Sew around this circle of four beads once more, and then through the 3D again. Following the thread path, weave through the daisy until you exit the D at the tip of the B bead on the opposite side.

STAGE 12 Pick up 1F and 4D. Sew through the attachment ring on one half of the clasp. Pick up 4D and sew down through the F and then through the D at the tip of the daisy. Sew around this loop of beads twice more for strength. Weave through the daisy and the tile until you exit the D at the tip of the middle picot along the opposite side of the tile (as shown in stage 16).

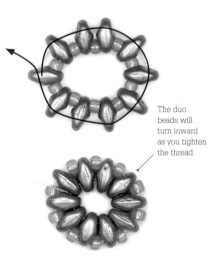

Sew around the loop three times.

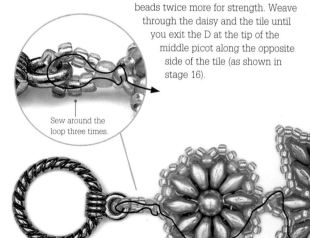

Finished length:
7 in. (18cm) including clasp

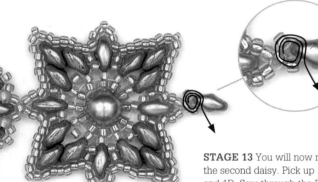

STAGE 13 You will now make the second daisy. Pick up 1D, 1B, and 1D. Sew through the D at the tip of the picot on the tile. Sew around this circle of four beads once more, and then again through the first D and B.

STAGE 16 Pick up 1D and sew through the D at the tip of the middle picot of the second tile. Pick up 1D and sew through the B in the daisy. Sew through this circle of beads once more, then weave through the tile to exit the D at the tip of the middle picot on the opposite side.

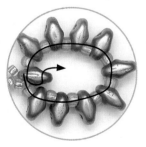

STAGE 14 Pick up [1F, 1B] nine times and 1F. Sew through the B from stage 13 to form a circle. Step up by sewing back through the empty hole of the same B.

STAGE 17 Repeat stages 13–16 once more to add one more daisy and tile, then repeat stages 13–15 once again to add the final daisy.

STAGE 18 Pick up 3D and sew back through the B below and then again through the first 2D. Add the second half of the clasp as before (stage 12). Weave in and fasten off the remaining thread and the beginning tail.

STAGE 15 Repeat stages 8–9 to form the center of the daisy. *Pick up 3D and sew through the next F.** Repeat from * to ** three more times. Sew through the next B and F. Repeat from * to ** four more times.

Summer Stars Necklace

Light up your look with this stunning star motif necklace, with crystal accents to make it shine from every angle. It really is the star of the show!

Finished length:
21 in. (53cm) including clasp

YOU WILL NEED (beads shown actual size)

BEAD BOX

- **A** = 8g duo beads, pink

- **B** = 11g 11º seed beads, aqua

- **C** = Forty-two 4mm faceted crystal beads, blue

- **D** = Eight 8mm faceted crystal beads, blue

- **E** = One 6 x 11mm vertical-drilled faceted crystal drop bead, blue

HARDWARE
- 29 ft. (8.8m) thread
- Toggle clasp

TOOLKIT
- Size 11 or 12 beading needle
- Scissors

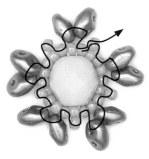

STAGE 1 Stages 1–6 form the star motif. Thread the needle with 3 ft. (90cm) of thread and pick up 20B. Sew through all the beads again in the same direction to form a circle and tie a knot to secure, leaving a tail of thread to weave in later. Sew through the first 5B again and gently tug the knot inside the beads.

STAGE 2 Pick up 1D and sew through the B opposite the B just exited. Sew back through the D and the first B. Sew through these three beads once more, and then through the next B in the circle.

STAGE 3 *Pick up 1B, skip the next B in the circle, and sew through the next B. Pick up 2A, skip the next B in the circle, and sew through the next B.** Repeat from * to ** four more times, then sew through the first B added in this stage. Don't worry if the motif looks a little messy; it will straighten in the next stage.

STAGE 4 *Pick up 2B and sew through the empty hole of the next A. Pick up 1A and sew through the next A. Pick up 2B and sew through the next B from stage 3.** Repeat from * to ** four more times, then sew through the first 2B added in this stage.

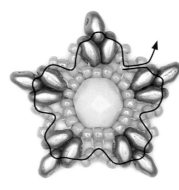

STAGE 5 *Pick up 3B and sew through the empty hole of the next A. Pick up 3B and sew through the next 5B from stages 2–3.** Repeat from * to ** four more times, then sew through the first 3B added in this stage.

STAGE 6 *Pick up 4B and sew back through the A and the first 2B just added. Pick up 1B and sew through the next 2B just added to form a picot. Sew through the next 3B from stage 5. Pick up 1C and sew through the next 3B from stage 5.** Repeat from * to ** four more times. Weave the remaining thread through the beads, knotting 4–5 times in between as you go, and then trim. Make six more stars (seven in total) and set aside.

STAGE 7 You will now start making the first section of the neck strap. Thread the needle with 5 ft. (1.5m) of thread. Pick up 9B and 1A. Sew through all the beads again to form a circle, and secure with a knot. Sew through the first 5B again and tug the knot inside the beads.

STAGE 8 Pick up 4B and sew through the attachment ring on one half of the clasp. Pick up 3B and sew down through the first of the 4B and then through the middle B from stage 7. Sew around this loop of beads three more times for strength. Weave through the beads from stage 7 until you exit the A.

Sew around the loop four times.

STAGE 9 Pick up 2B and sew through the empty hole of the A. Pick up 2B and sew through the first hole of the A. Sew through the first 2B and the second hole of the A again.

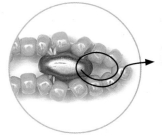

STAGE 10 Pick up 5B and sew through the second hole of the A to form a circle. Sew through the first 3B again.

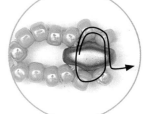

STAGE 11 Pick up 2B, 1A, and 2B. Sew through the B just exited to form a circle. Sew through the first 2B and the A again.

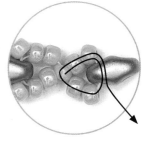

STAGE 12 Repeat stages 9–11 once more, then stage 9 once again. You will now have a string of three duo bead links on the neck strap.

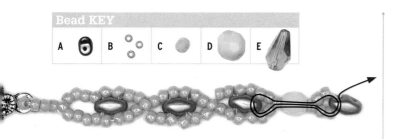

Bead KEY

A | B | C | D | E

STAGE 13 Now add a crystal (C) to the links of the neck strap (see technique at the bottom of page 45).

STAGE 14 Repeat stages 9–13 once more, then stages 9–12 once again. This completes the first section of the neck strap.

STAGE 15 You will now join the star motifs to the neck strap. Pick up 2B and sew up through the B at the top left point of the first star. Pick up 2B and sew through the last A of the neck strap and the first 2B added in this stage. Sew through the B at the point of the star again, then weave through the beads of the star to exit the B at the top right point.

STAGE 16 Pick up 2B, 1A, and 2B. Sew down through the B at the point of the star and then through the first 2B and A just added. Pick up 2B and sew through the empty hole of the A. Pick up 2B and sew through the first hole of the A, the next 2B, and the second hole of the A. Pick up 2B and sew up through the B at the top left point of the second star motif. Pick up 2B and sew through the A and the next 2B toward the second star. Sew through the B at the point of the second star again. Weave through the beads of the second star to exit the top right point. Continue joining all the star motifs together in this way, until you exit the top right point of the final star.

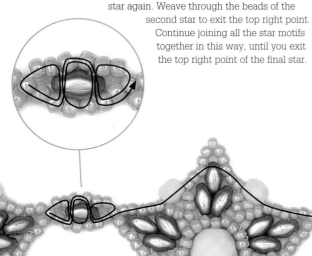

STAGE 17 Make another section of neck strap to match the first and attach the other half of the clasp. Weave in and fasten off the thread as before.

STAGE 18 To make the half-motif for the drop pendant, thread the needle with 3 ft. (90cm) of thread and pick up 20B. Sew through all the beads again to form a circle, and secure with a knot. Sew through the first 5B again and tug the knot inside the beads.

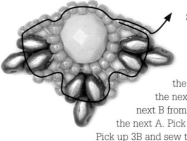

STAGE 19 Pick up 1D and sew through the B opposite the B just exited. Sew back through the D and the first B. Sew through these three beads once more, and then through the next 3B in the circle.

STAGE 20 *Pick up 1B, skip the next B in the circle, and sew through the next B. Pick up 1A, skip the next B in the circle, and sew through the next B.** Repeat from * to ** twice more. Pick up 1B, skip the next B in the circle, and sew through the remaining beads in the circle to exit the first B added in this stage.

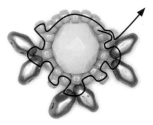

STAGE 21 Pick up 3B and sew through the empty hole of the next A. Pick up 1A and sew through the next A. Pick up 2B and sew through the B from stage 20. Pick up 2B and sew through the next A. Pick up 1A and sew through the next A. Pick up 2B and sew through the next B from stage 20. Pick up 2B and sew through the next A. Pick up 1A and sew through the next A. Pick up 3B and sew through the next B from stage 20. Sew through the remaining beads in the circle to exit the first 3B added in this stage.

STAGE 22 *Pick up 3B and sew through the empty hole of the next A. Pick up 3B and sew through the next 5B beads from stages 20–21.** Repeat from * to ** twice more. Sew through the remaining beads in the circle to exit the first 3B added in this stage.

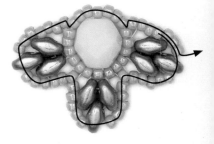

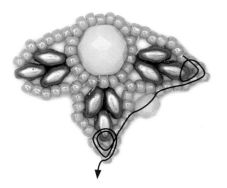

STAGE 23 *Pick up 4B and sew back through the A and the first 2B just added. Pick up 1B and sew through the next 2B just added to form a picot.** Sew through the next 3B from stage 22. Pick up 1C and sew through the next 3B from stage 22. Repeat from * to ** once more to form a picot at the bottom of the half-motif. Sew back through the A and 3B of the picot to exit the bottom point of the motif.

STAGE 24 Now attach the crystal drop to the bottom of the half-motif (see technique below). After sewing back through the B at the bottom point of the motif, sew up through the next 5B on the left side. Pick up 1C and sew through the next 3B from stage 22. Repeat stage 23 from * to ** to form a picot at the left point of the motif. Sew through the next 11B across the top of the motif.

STAGE 25 Now make a link to attach the pendant to the necklace. Pick up 2B, 1A, and 2B. Sew back through the B at the top the motif and then through the first 2B and A just added. Pick up 2B and sew through the empty hole of the A. Pick up 2B and sew through the first hole of the A, the next 2B, and the second hole of the A. Pick up 5B and sew through the A and the first 3B just added.

STAGE 26 Pick up 3B and sew through the C on the lowest side of the middle star motif in the necklace. Pick up 3B and sew through the B just exited at the top of the pendant link. Sew through these beads once or twice more, then weave in and fasten off the thread. Do the same with any tail threads.

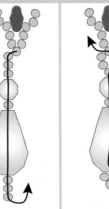

TECHNIQUES: ADDING A CRYSTAL TO THE NECK STRAP (STAGE 13)

STEP 1
After exiting the last A in the neck strap, pick up 3B, 1C, 3B, 1A, and 2B.

STEP 2
Skip the last five beads picked up and sew back through 1B, 1C, and 1B. Pick up 2B and sew through the A in the neck strap. Sew back through the beads of the crystal link to exit the A just added.

ATTACHING THE CRYSTAL DROP (STAGE 24)

STEP 1
After exiting the B at the bottom point of the half-star motif, pick up 3B, 1C, 1B, 1E, and 3B.

STEP 2
Skip the last 3B picked up and sew back up through 1E, 1B, 1C, and 1B. Pick up 2B and sew through the B at the bottom of the half-motif.

Grow as you go

These projects are made on a continuous thread, finishing one motif or section and then immediately moving on to the next, so your project grows as you go. The Santi Drop Earrings (page 58) demonstrate how to continue adding embellishments to a motif to create a whole new design.

New Leaf Necklace

Leaves are always a popular motif in all types of jewelry, and this fabulous necklace can be made in as many or as few colors as you wish. Here it is shown in resplendent fall colors, but you could use summer greens, spring pinks, or winter blues to reflect another season. The necklace is made in three parts: two chains of leaves worked from the center to the clasp, and one extra leaf used as a central pendant to join them.

Finished length:
21 in. (54cm) including clasp

YOU WILL NEED (beads shown actual size)

BEAD BOX
- **A** = 8g duo beads, red

- **B** = 7g duo beads, copper

- **C** = 7g duo beads, gold

- **D** = 6g 15º seed beads, bronze

- **E** = 2g 11º seed beads, bronze

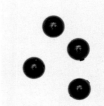

- **F** = Nineteen 6mm glass pearls, blackberry

HARDWARE
- 30 ft. (9.1m) thread
- Toggle clasp

TOOLKIT
- Size 11 or 12 beading needle
- Scissors
- Pliers

See it GROW

STAGE 1 Stages 1–8 form the first leaf. Thread the needle with a comfortable length of thread; 3 ft. (90cm) will complete two leaves. Pick up 1E, 1F, 1E, 5D, 1E, and 5D. Sew through all the beads again in the same direction to form a circle, leaving a tail of thread to weave in later. Sew through the first E, F, and E again.

STAGE 2 Pick up [1A, 1E] four times and 1A. Sew through the first E, F, and E from stage 1. Sew through all these beads once more.

STAGE 3 Pick up 3D and sew through the empty hole of the first A. Pick up 1A and sew through the next A. [Pick up 2A and sew through the next A] twice. Pick up 1A and sew through the next A. Pick up 3D and sew through the E, F, and E from stage 1, and then through the first 3D added in this stage.

STAGE 4 Pick up 3D and sew through the empty hole of the first A from stage 3. Pick up 3D and sew through the next A. Pick up 1A and sew through the next A. Pick up 2A and sew through the next A. Pick up 1A and sew through the next A. Pick up 3D and sew through the next A. Pick up 3D and sew through the next 3D, 1E, 1F, 1E, 6D, 1A, and 3D.

STAGE 5 [Pick up 3D and sew through the next A] twice. Pick up 1A and sew through the next A. Pick up 3D and sew through the next A. Pick up 3D and sew through the next 3D, 1A, 6D, 1E, 1F, 1E, and 6D. You may need to use pliers to grip the needle and pull it through as the beads begin to fill with thread.

STAGE 6 You will now shape the leaf by making picots around it. *Pick up 4D and sew back through the A and the first 2D just added. Pick up 1D and sew through the next 2D just added to form a picot.** Sew through the next 6D. Repeat from * to ** once more to make the second picot. Sew through the next 3D.

STAGE 7 To make the larger picot at the top of the leaf, pick up 3D and sew through the empty hole of the next A. Pick up 4D and sew through the A again and the first 2D just added. Pick up 1E and sew through the next 2D just added and the A again. Pick up 3D and sew down through the next 3D on leaf.

STAGE 8 Make two more picots on the second side of the leaf to match the first two added in stage 6. Following the thread path, weave through the beads to exit the E at the tip of the larger picot at the top of the leaf.

STAGE 9 To make the base of the second leaf, pick up 5D, 1E, 1F, 1E, and 5D. Sew through the E at the top of the first leaf to form a circle. Sew through the first 5D, 1E, 1F, and 1E again.

Alternate red, copper, and gold leaves.

Sew around the loop three times.

STAGE 10 To complete the second leaf, repeat stages 2–8 using B instead of A beads. To make the third leaf, repeat stage 9 and then stages 2–8 using C instead of A beads. Continue in this way to make a total of nine leaves following this color sequence. Refer to the technique below for how to start a new length of thread when you need to.

STAGE 11 You will now add one half of the clasp to the chain of nine leaves. Exiting the E at the top of the last leaf, pick up 1E and 4D. Sew through the attachment ring on one half of the clasp. Pick up 4D and sew down through the E just added and the E at the leaf tip. Sew around this loop of beads twice more for strength. Weave the remaining thread through the beads, knotting 4–5 times in between as you go, and then trim. Fasten off any other tails of thread in the same way.

STAGE 12 Make a second chain of nine leaves to match the first, and attach the second half of the clasp to the end of this one.

STAGE 13 Repeat stages 1–8 using A beads to make one more leaf for the central pendant, but this time do not weave through the beads to exit the picot at the top. Instead, weave through to exit the E at the base of the leaf.

Exit this E on the final pendant leaf.

TECHNIQUE: STARTING A NEW LENGTH OF THREAD

Whenever you need to start a new length of thread, fasten off the old thread after completing a stage 8, then start a new length of thread as described in stage 1. However, instead of picking up 1E between the two sets of 5D, you should sew through the E at the top of the previous leaf to join the two components together. You can then continue from stage 2 using the next color of duo beads in the sequence.

STAGE 14 You will now join the three parts of the necklace together. Pick up 1E and sew through the E at the base of the leaf at the bottom of the first chain. Pick up 1E and sew through the E at the base of the leaf at the bottom of the second chain. Pick up 1E and sew through the E at the base of the pendant leaf. Sew through this circle of E beads several times tightly. Weave in and fasten off the thread.

Demi Tuile Bracelet

This simple, quick-to-make bracelet has lots of sparkle and elegance. It is made from a series of half-motifs, worked on only one side of the faceted crystal bead. You could use glass pearls instead of crystals if you prefer.

Finished length: 7½ in. (19cm) including clasp

See it GROW

STAGE 1 Stages 1–5 form the first half-motif. Thread the needle with a comfortable length of thread. The bracelet can be made from start to finish on a 6 ft. (1.8m) length of thread, but you can use a shorter length, fasten off, and start a new one partway through if you prefer. Pick up 1C and 10B. Sew through all the beads again in the same direction to form a circle and tie a knot to secure, leaving a tail of thread to weave in later. Sew through the C again and gently tug the knot inside the beads.

STAGE 2 Pick up [1B, 2A] three times and 1B. Sew through the C again. Sew through all of the beads just added and the C once more, and then through the first B again.

STAGE 3 Pick up 2B and sew through the empty hole of the next A. [Pick up 1A and sew through the next A. Pick up 1D and sew through the next A] twice. Pick up 1A and sew through the next A. Pick up 2B and sew through the next 1B, 1C, and 3B, so that you exit the second B added in this stage.

STAGE 4 Pick up 3B and sew through the empty hole of the next A. [Pick up 2B and sew through the next D. Pick up 2B and sew through the next A] twice. Pick up 3B and sew through the next 3B, 1C, and 6B, so that you exit the third B added in this stage.

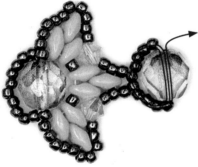

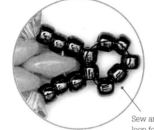

Sew around the loop four times.

Attach the clasp using a jump ring.

STAGE 5 Pick up 3B and sew through the next 2B, 1D, and 2B. Pick up 4B and sew through the next 2B, 1D, and 2B. Pick up 3B and sew through the next 6B and 1C. Following the thread path, weave through the outer beads until you exit the 2B at the tip of the middle point on the motif (the third B of the 4B added in this stage).

STAGE 6 To start the next half-motif, pick up 4B, 1C, and 4B. Sew through the 2B at the tip of the middle point on the first half-motif to form a circle. Sew through the circle of beads once more, and then through the first 4B and 1C again.

STAGE 7 Repeat stages 2–6 until you have eight half-motifs in total, omitting stage 6 on the last one. To add a loop of beads for attaching the clasp, pick up 5B and sew through the 2B at the tip of the last motif to form a circle. Sew around this loop of beads three more times for strength. Weave the remaining thread through the beads, knotting 4–5 times in between as you go, and then trim. Weave in and fasten off the beginning tail in the same way.

STAGE 8 Using jump rings, attach the clasp securely to the loops at each end of the bracelet.

YOU WILL NEED (beads shown actual size)

BEAD BOX
* **A** = 6g duo beads, beige

* **B** = 4g 11º seed beads, bronze

* **C** = Eight 8mm faceted crystal beads, aqua

* **D** = Sixteen 4mm crystal bicones, blue

HARDWARE
* 6 ft. (1.8m) thread
* Toggle clasp
* Two 4mm or 6mm jump rings

TOOLKIT
* Size 11 or 12 beading needle
* Scissors
* Pliers

Daisy Chain Bracelet

Is it a flower bracelet or a spiral? The illusion of two strands of duo beads twisted around each other is achieved simply by weaving the beads around the central glass pearls using a clever combination of two colors. It is advisable to use quality glass pearls for this bracelet. Some glass pearls have an indentation at each end where the hole goes through, making them less than perfectly round, and this can distort the shape of the bracelet a little.

Finished length:
7½ in. (19cm) including clasp

YOU WILL NEED (beads shown actual size)

BEAD BOX
- **A** = 5g duo beads, blue

- **B** = 5g duo beads, cream

- **C** = 2g 11º seed beads, bronze

- **D** = Nine 6mm glass pearls, gold

HARDWARE
- 9 ft. (2.7m) thread
- Toggle clasp

TOOLKIT
- Size 11 or 12 beading needle
- Scissors

STAGE 1 Thread the needle with a comfortable length of thread; 3 ft. (90cm) will complete three daisies. Pick up 6A and 6B. Sew through all the beads again in the same direction to form a circle, leaving a tail of thread to weave in later. Sew through the first A again.

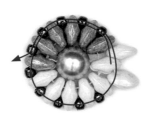

STAGE 2 Pick up 1D and sew through the B opposite the A just exited. Sew back through the D and A, and then through the D and opposite B again. Step up by sewing back through the empty hole of the same B.

STAGE 3 Pick up 1B and sew through the empty hole of the next A. [Pick up 1C and sew through the next duo bead] ten times. Pick up 1B and sew through the next 2B. Continue around the outer beads of the daisy until you exit the fifth C added in this stage.

STAGE 4 Pick up 3C and sew back through the A below. Sew through the first 2C just added.

Exit this B at the end of stage 5.

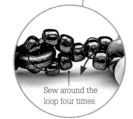

Sew around the loop four times.

STAGE 5 Pick up 4C and sew through the attachment ring on one half of the clasp. Pick up 3C and sew down through the first of the 4C and then through the C at the tip of the daisy. Sew around this loop of beads three more times for strength. Weave through the beads around the bottom of the daisy until you exit the last B.

STAGE 6 Pick up 2C and sew back through the empty hole of the B just exited. Pick up 1B and sew through the next B. Pick up 2C and sew through the 3B at the end of the daisy, the first 2C added in this stage, and the next 2B. Step up through the B just exited.

STAGE 7 Pick up 5B and 6A. Sew through the B just exited and then through all these beads again, to exit the same B as before.

STAGE 8 Pick up 1D and sew through the A opposite the B just exited. Sew back through the D and B, and then through the D and opposite A again. Step up through the same A.

STAGE 9 Pick up 1A and sew through the empty hole of the next B. [Pick up 1C and sew through the next B] four times. Sew through the next 3B and 1A. [Pick up 1C and sew through the next A] four times. Pick up 1A and sew through the next 2A.

Bead KEY

A · B · C · D

STAGE 13 Pick up 1B and sew through the empty hole of the next A. [Pick up 1C and sew through the next A] four times. Sew through the next 3A and 1B. [Pick up 1C and sew through the next B] four times. Pick up 1B and sew through the next 2B.

STAGE 10 Pick up 2C and sew back through the empty hole of the A just exited. Pick up 1A and sew through the next A. Pick up 2C and sew through the 3A at the end of the daisy, the first 2C added in this stage, and the next 2A. Step up through the A just exited.

STAGE 14 Repeat stages 6–13 twice more, and then stages 6–12 once again, to make a chain of nine daisies in total.

STAGE 11 Pick up 5A and 6B. Sew through the A just exited and then through all these beads again, to exit the same A as before.

STAGE 15 [Pick up 1C and sew through the empty hole of the next A] five times. Sew through the next 3A and 1B. [Pick up 1C and sew through the next B] five times, to exit the last B at the end of the daisy chain.

STAGE 16 Attach the second half of the clasp as before (stages 4–5). Weave the remaining thread through the beads, knotting 4–5 times in between as you go, and then trim. Weave in and fasten off the beginning tail in the same way.

STAGE 12 Pick up 1D and sew through the B opposite the A just exited. Sew back through the D and A, and then through the D and opposite B again. Step up through the same B.

Finished length:
19 in. (48cm) including clasp

Mimosa Necklace

Little clusters of glass pearls and duo beads give this necklace a touch of Bollywood glamor, draping around the neck like fruits on a vine. The necklace is made one cluster at a time, linked together with sparkling crystal beads.

YOU WILL NEED (beads shown actual size)

BEAD BOX

- **A** = 11g duo beads, blue

- **B** = Eighty-four 4mm glass pearls, gold

- **C** = Twenty 4mm faceted crystal beads, blue

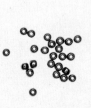

- **D** = 11g 11º seed beads, bronze

HARDWARE
- 33 ft. (10m) thread
- Toggle clasp

TOOLKIT
- Size 11 or 12 beading needle
- Scissors

See it GROW

Bead KEY			
A	B	C	D

STAGE 1 Stages 1–4 form the first motif. Thread the needle with a comfortable length of thread; 3 ft. (90cm) will complete two motifs. Pick up [1B, 1D] four times. Sew through all the beads again in the same direction to form a circle and tie a knot to secure, leaving a 12 in. (30cm) tail for attaching the clasp later. Sew through the first four beads again and gently tug the knot inside the beads.

STAGE 2 *Pick up 5D, skip the next B, and sew through the next D.** Repeat from * to ** twice more. Pick up 6A, skip the next B, and sew through the next 2D.

STAGE 3 *Pick up 1D and sew through the empty hole of the next A.** Repeat from * to ** twice more. Pick up 1A and sew through the next A. Repeat from * to ** twice more. Pick up 1D and sew through the 2D, 1B, and 2D across the center of the motif. Sew through the first D added in this stage.

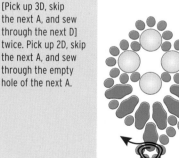

STAGE 4 Referring to the technique panel below, add D beads around the bottom half of the motif, with a picot at the bottom point, then weave across the center of the motif to exit the D bead shown (the fourth D added in stage 2).

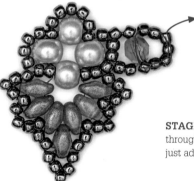

STAGE 5 You will now make the first crystal link. Pick up 2D, 1C, and 2D. Sew up through the middle 3D of the first 5D from stage 2. Sew through the first 2D and 1C just added.

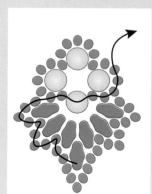

STAGE 6 Pick up 7D and sew through the C and the first 5D just added.

TECHNIQUE: ADDING THE OUTER BEADS AND PICOT (STAGE 4)

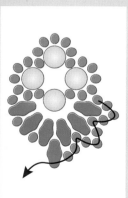

STEP 1
[Pick up 3D, skip the next A, and sew through the next D] twice. Pick up 2D, skip the next A, and sew through the empty hole of the next A.

STEP 2
To form the picot at the bottom point of the motif, pick up 4D and sew back through the A and the first 2D just added. Pick up 1D and sew through the second 2D just added and the A again.

STEP 3
Pick up 2D, skip the next A, and sew through the next D. [Pick up 3D, skip the next A, and sew through the next D] twice. Sew through the 2D, 1B, and 2D across the center of the motif, and then through the next 3D around the right-hand B.

Make 21 motifs to
match sample shown.

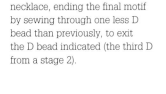

Exit this D on
the final motif to
attach the clasp.

STAGE 7 Stages 7–10 form the second motif. Pick
up 1D, 1B, and 1D. Sew up through the middle 3D
of the 7D from stage 6, and then through the first D
and B added in this stage.

STAGE 11 Repeat stages 5–10
until there are 21 motifs on the
necklace, ending the final motif
by sewing through one less D
bead than previously, to exit
the D bead indicated (the third D
from a stage 2).

STAGE 8 Pick up [1D, 1B] three times and 1D.
Sew down through the B from stage 7 and then
through the first D, B, and D added in this stage.

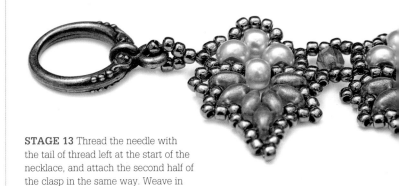

STAGE 12 Pick up 4D and sew
through the attachment ring on one
half of the clasp. Pick up 3D and sew
down through the first of the 4D and
then through the D on the motif. Sew
around this loop of beads three more
times for strength. Weave the remaining
thread through the beads, knotting 4–5 times
in between as you go, and then trim.

Sew around the
loop four times.

STAGE 9 *Pick up 5D,
skip the next B, and sew
through the next D.**
Repeat from * to ** once
more. Sew through the
6D surrounding the next
B. Pick up 6A, skip the
next B, and sew through
the next 2D.

STAGE 13 Thread the needle with
the tail of thread left at the start of the
necklace, and attach the second half of
the clasp in the same way. Weave in
and fasten off the thread.

STAGE 10 Repeat stages 3–4 once more to complete the second motif.

Finished length: 2½ in. (6.5cm) excluding ear hook

Santi Drop Earrings

YOU WILL NEED
(beads shown actual size)

BEAD BOX
• **A** = 2g duo beads, blue

• **B** = Eighteen 4mm glass pearls, ivory

• **C** = 2g 11º seed beads, silver

• **D** = 1g 15º seed beads, silver

• **E** = Two 7 x 10mm vertical-drilled pearl drop beads, ivory

HARDWARE
• 6 ft. (1.8m) thread
• Pair of ear hooks

TOOLKIT
• Size 11 or 12 beading needle
• Scissors
• Pliers

Santi Drop Earrings

Using the motif from the Mimosa Necklace (page 55) as a starting point, these earrings demonstrate how to expand and adapt a design with further beaded embellishments to produce a very different look. It would be easy to make a third motif and attach a bail to use as a matching pendant. You could also use a crystal drop bead instead of a pearl for extra sparkle.

Dashed line indicates the seven "pass" beads.

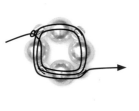

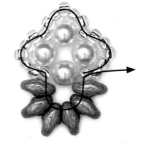

STAGE 1 Thread the needle with 3 ft. (90cm) of thread. Pick up [1B, 1C] four times. Sew through all the beads again in the same direction to form a circle and tie a knot to secure, leaving a tail of thread to weave in later. Sew through the first four beads again and gently tug the knot inside.

STAGE 2 *Pick up 5C, skip the next B, and sew through the next C.* Repeat from * to ** twice more. Pick up 6A, skip the next B, and sew through the next 2C.

STAGE 3 *Pick up 1C and sew through the empty hole of the next A.** Repeat from * to ** five more times. Pick up 1C and sew through the 2C, 1B, and 2C across the center of the motif. Sew through the first C added in this stage. Note: The last seven beads will now be referred to as the "pass" beads, as you will be passing through them several times.

STAGE 4 Pick up 3C, skip the next A, and sew through the next C.** Repeat from * to ** five more times. Sew through the pass beads and the first 2C added in this stage.

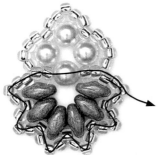

STAGE 5 *Pick up 1B, skip the next 3C, and sew through the next C.** Repeat from * to ** four more times. Sew through the next C, the pass beads, the next 2C from stage 4, and the first B added in this stage.

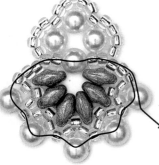

STAGE 6 Pick up 1A and sew through the next B. Pick up 1C and 1A, and sew through the next B. Pick up 1A and 1C, and sew through the next B. Pick up 1A and sew through the next B. Sew through the next 2C, the pass beads, and the next 2C from stage 4.

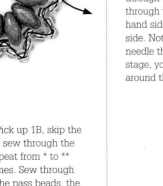

STAGE 7 Pick up 6C and sew through the empty hole of the next A. Pick up 5C and sew through the next A. Pick up 2A and sew through the next A. Pick up 5C and sew through the next A. Pick up 6C and sew through the next 2C and the pass beads. Continue around the outer beads until you exit the last C on the bottom right of the motif.

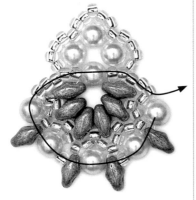

STAGE 8 Pick up 2C and sew through the empty hole of the next A from stage 7. Pick up 1A and sew through the next A. Pick up 2C and sew up through the outer beads on the left-hand side of the motif. Continue through the pass beads and then down through the outer beads on the right-hand side, to exit the last C on that side. Note: If you struggle to get the needle through the pass beads by this stage, you can sew through the C beads around the top four pearls instead.

STAGE 9 Pick up 2C and sew through the empty hole of the bottom A. Pick up 4C and sew back through the A and the first 2C just added. Pick up 1C and sew through the next 2C just added to form a picot. Sew back through the A and next 3C so that you exit the C at the bottom tip of the motif.

STAGE 10 Pick up 3C, 1E, and 3C. Skip the last 3C and sew back up through the E and next 3C. Sew back through the C at the tip of the motif, and then up through the 2C on the right side of the picot. Sew back through the bottom A toward the left-hand side of the motif. Pick up 2C and sew up through the outer beads of the motif until you exit the center C bead at the top.

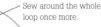
Sew around the whole loop once more.

STAGE 11 Pick up 8D and sew through the center C on the motif and the first 4D just added. Pick up 1D and sew through the next 4D just added and the center C. Sew around this loop of beads once more for strength. Weave the remaining thread through the beads, knotting 4–5 times in between as you go, and then trim. Weave in and fasten off the beginning tail in the same way. Make a second earring to match and add an ear hook to the beaded loops at the top.

Cascara Bangle

Everyone loves a bangle, and this one will be no exception. Made from an outer band featuring a shell pattern and a plain inner band, it will brighten any outfit, day or evening wear, and could be made with crystal bicones instead of pearls for added sparkle. To make the correct size, tuck your thumb behind your fingers as if you were putting on a bangle and measure around your knuckles. The sample shown is for a measurement of 7½ in. (19cm) and consists of 19 shells on the outer band. So for every extra ⅜ in. (1cm) needed, add one shell; for every ⅜ in. (1cm) less, subtract one shell.

Finished inside diameter:
7½ in. (19cm)

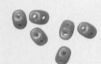

STAGE 1 Thread the needle with a comfortable length of thread; 3 ft. (90cm) will complete five outer shell units. Pick up 1C, 1D, 1C, and 5A. Sew through all the beads again in the same direction to form a circle and tie a knot to secure, leaving a tail of thread to weave in later. Sew through the first C, D, and C again and gently tug the knot inside the beads.

STAGE 2 Pick up 2C and sew through the empty hole of the next A. [Pick up 1C and sew through the next A] four times. Pick up 2C and sew through the C, D, and C from stage 1. Continue around the outer beads until you exit the fifth C added in this stage. This completes the first shell of the outer band.

STAGE 3 To add the second shell, pick up 2C, 1D, and 2C. Sew up through the middle C, A, and C on the first shell, and then through the first 2C and D just added.

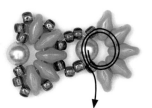

STAGE 4 Pick up 1C, 5A, and 1C, and sew down through the D from stage 3. Sew through all the beads once more and then through the first C just added.

STAGE 5 Pick up 2C and sew through the empty hole of the next A. [Pick up 1C and sew through the next A] four times. Pick up 2C and sew through the next C, D, and C from stages 3–4. Continue around the outer beads of the second shell until you exit the fifth C added in this stage. This completes the second shell.

STAGE 6 Repeat stages 3–5 to make 19 shells in total.

STAGE 7 To join the two ends of the strip of shells together, pick up 2C and sew through the D on the first shell, taking care not to twist the shells. Pick up 2C and sew through the middle C, A, and C on the last shell. Sew through all the beads once more, then weave down through the first shell to exit the third C added in stage 2. (Weave in and fasten off the beginning tail thread if you have not already done so.)

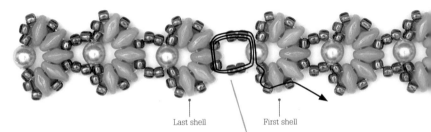

Last shell   First shell

Note

The two ends of the strip of shells are joined together in stage 7, so that you will finish this stage with a circular band of shells. However, note that stages 7–15 have been demonstrated as flat sections of beading for clarity. For each of these stages, simply follow the instructions to work around the whole of the circular band.

YOU WILL NEED (beads shown actual size)

BEAD BOX
- **A** = 7g duo beads, blue
- **B** = 20g duo beads, gold
- **C** = 4g 11º seed beads, blue
- **D** = Fifty-seven 4mm glass pearls, gold

HARDWARE
- 22 ft. (6.6m) thread

TOOLKIT
- Size 11 or 12 beading needle
- Scissors
- Pliers

See it GROW

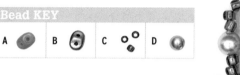

Dashed lines indicate the thread continuing around the circumference of the bangle.

STAGE 8 You will now add an edging of beads around the bottom of the shell band. *Pick up 1C, 1D, and 1C. Sew through the C before the first A on the next shell, then through the next A and C of the same shell.** Repeat from * to ** all the way around the bottom edge, then sew through the first C, D, and C added in this stage.

STAGE 9 Weave up through the fan of A and C beads on the next shell until you exit the C after the last A on the top edge of the shell band.

STAGE 10 Add an edging around the top of the shell band to match the bottom edge (stage 8). At this point you may prefer to finish the thread and attach a new one.

STAGE 11 Weave down through the beads on the "straight" side of the next shell until you exit the C before the first A on the bottom edge.

STAGE 12 You will now add the first row of beads for the inner band of the bangle (see also technique below). *Pick up 1C, 1B, and 1C. Skip the A and sew through the next C of the same shell. Pick up 1B, skip the next C of the edging, and sew through the D. Pick up 1B, skip the next C of the edging, and sew through the C of the next shell immediately before the first A.** Repeat from * to ** all the way around. Sew through the first C and B added in this stage, then step up by sewing back through the empty hole of the same B. Note that the beads may look a little messy at this stage, but they will straighten as you add the next few rows.

**TECHNIQUE:
DIAGRAM VIEW OF
THE INNER BAND**

An open view showing the formation of the inner band and how it is attached to the outer shell band along each edge. Note that at stage 15, the inner band will actually be behind the shells.

STAGE 12

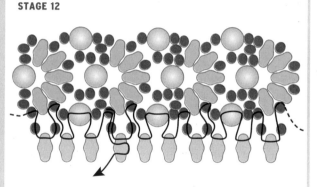

STAGE 13

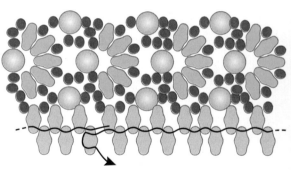

The bangle will look like
this at the end of stage 12.

Tip Keeping the thread tight
You may find the beads relaxing on the thread a little when adding each row of beads for the inner band. To keep the thread tight, when you reach the end of each row, sew again through the first few beads of the row and tie a half-hitch knot between the beads to hold the thread in place. Then sew through the next B of the row and step up, ready to add the following row of beads.

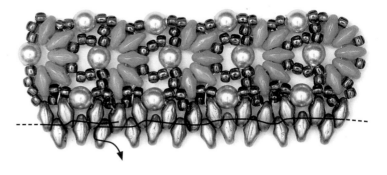

STAGE 13 *Pick up 1B and sew through the empty hole of the next B.** Repeat from * to ** all the way around. Sew through the first B added in this stage, then step up through the same B (refer to the tip above if you find the beads becoming loose on the thread).

REVERSE
SIDE

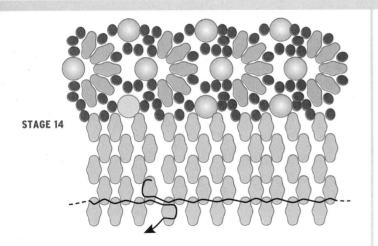

STAGE 14 Repeat stage 13 three more times until there are five rows of B beads. Step up as before.

STAGE 15 Carefully flip the band of B beads inside the shell band, making sure none of the beads becomes tucked inside, especially the C beads. If so, lever them up gently with a bead awl or your needle. Taking care to match the bead pattern along the opposite edge of the bangle, use C beads to attach the last row of B beads to the shell band (see stage 12 and technique below). You may need to use pliers to ease the needle through some of the more awkward angles. Weave in and fasten off the remaining thread.

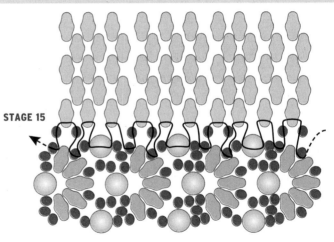

STAGE 14

STAGE 15

Diamond Twist Bracelet

This bracelet cleverly gives the appearance of two intersecting strands of duo beads, with neat lines of color forming the diamond shapes around faceted crystal beads. Glass pearls can be used instead of crystals if you prefer. The bracelet is made in three main phases, starting with the central strip of crystals, which form the foundation for working the points of the diamonds along the bottom and then the top.

Finished length: 7 in. (18cm) including clasp

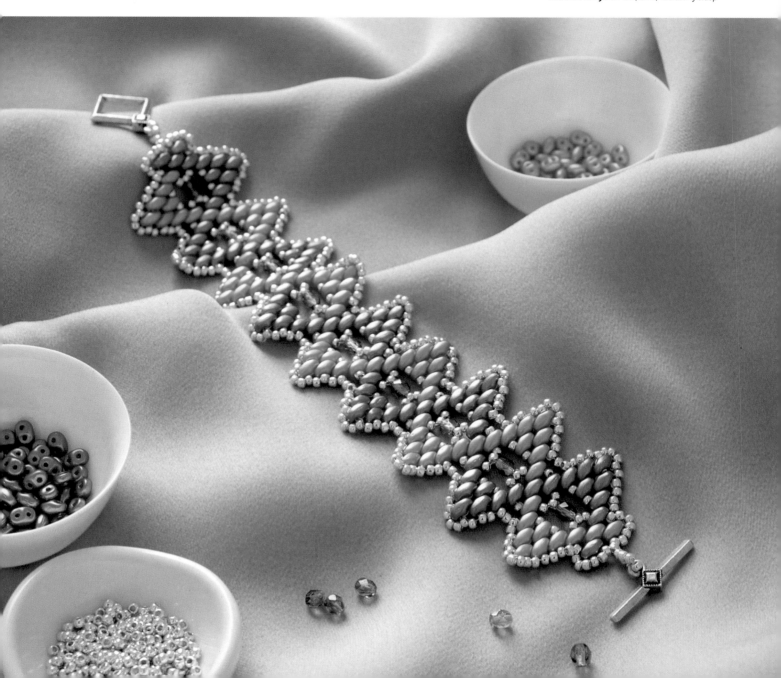

STAGE 1 Stages 1–10 form the foundation strip of beads running along the center of the bracelet. Thread the needle with a comfortable length of thread; you will need to fasten off and attach new threads as you progress. Add a stop bead, leaving a 12 in. (30cm) tail for attaching the clasp later. Pick up 1A, 2B, 3C, and 1A. Sew back through the empty hole of the first B picked up.

STAGE 2 Pick up 1B and 3C. Following the thread path, sew through all the beads from stage 1 again and then continue around until you exit the middle of the 3C added in stage 1.

STAGE 3 Pick up 1D and 1C. Sew back through the D and the middle C from stage 1, and then again through the D and C just added.

STAGE 4 Pick up 1C, 1B, 2A, 3C, and 1B. Sew back through the empty hole of the first A just added.

STAGE 5 Pick up 1A and 1C. Sew through the C from stage 3, and then through the first 1C, 1B, 2A, and 2C from stage 4, so that you exit the middle C at the end of the foundation.

STAGE 6 Pick up 1D and 1C. Sew back through the D and the middle C exited in stage 5, and then again through the D and C just added.

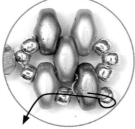

STAGE 7 Pick up 1C, 1A, 2B, 3C, and 1A. Sew back through the empty hole of the first B just added.

STAGE 8 Pick up 1B and 1C. Sew through the C from stage 6, and then through the first 1C, 1A, 2B, and 2C from stage 7.

STAGE 9 Repeat stages 3–8 three more times, and then stages 3–5 once again. On the final repeat of stage 5, sew through 3C instead of 2C at the end. Then sew through the next B, and step up by sewing back through the empty hole of the same B.

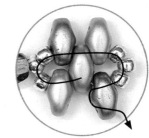

STAGE 10 C beads are now used as "turn" beads for sewing back and forth to create the bottom points of the diamonds. Pick up 1C, turn, and sew back through the B just exited. Pick up 1C and sew through the empty hole of the next A.

YOU WILL NEED (beads shown actual size)

BEAD BOX
- **A** = 6g duo beads, blue

- **B** = 6g duo beads, lilac

- **C** = 4g 11° seed beads, silver

- **D** = Nine 4mm faceted crystal beads, gray

HARDWARE
- 18 ft. (5.4m) thread
- Toggle clasp

TOOLKIT
- Size 11 or 12 beading needle
- Scissors
- Pliers
- Stop bead

Bead KEY

A	B	C	D
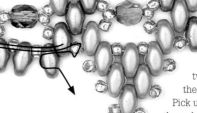			

STAGE 11 You will now start forming the first diamond point. Pick up [1A, 1C] twice and 1A. Sew through the empty hole of the next A. Pick up 1C, turn, and sew back through the A just exited, all of the beads just added, and the next A and C of the foundation. Turn and sew back through 2A. Step up by sewing back through the empty hole of the A just exited.

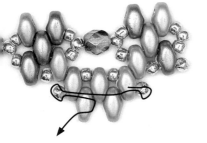

STAGE 12 Pick up 1C, turn, and sew back through the A just exited. [Pick up 1A and sew through the next A] twice. Pick up 1C, turn, and sew back through the next 2A. Step up through the A just exited.

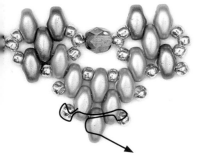

STAGE 13 Pick up 1C, turn, and sew back through the A just exited. Pick up 1A and sew through the next A. Pick up 1C, turn, and sew back through the next 2A. Step up through the A just exited.

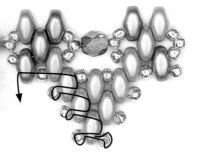

STAGE 14 Pick up 1C, turn, and sew back through the A just exited. Pick up 1C, turn, and sew back through the same A. Weave up through the A beads along the left edge of the diamond, using the C beads to turn, and then sew through the next A, C, and B of the foundation.

STAGE 15 You will now start forming the second diamond point. Pick up [1B, 1C] twice and 1B. Sew through the empty hole of the next B. Pick up 1C, turn, and sew back through the B just exited, all of the beads just added, and the next B and C of the foundation. Turn and sew back through 2B. Step up through the B just exited.

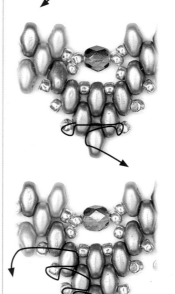

STAGE 16 Pick up 1C, turn, and sew back through the B just exited. [Pick up 1B and sew through the next B] twice. Pick up 1C, turn, and sew back through the next 2B. Step up through the B just exited.

STAGE 17 Pick up 1C, turn, and sew back through the B just exited. Pick up 1B and sew through the next B. Pick up 1C, turn, and sew back through the next 2B. Step up through the B just exited.

STAGE 18 Pick up 1C, turn, and sew back through the B just exited. Pick up 1C, turn, and sew back through the same B. Weave up through the B beads along the left edge of the diamond, using the C beads to turn, and then sew through the next B, C, and A of the foundation.

STAGE 19 Repeat stages 11–18 three more times, and then stages 11–14 once again. This completes the diamond points along the bottom edge of the bracelet.

STAGE 20 Pick up 1C, turn, and sew back through the B just exited. Step up through the other hole of the same B. Sew through the 3C at the end of the foundation and the next A. Step up through the other hole of the same A. Pick up 1C, turn, and sew back through the A just exited. Pick up 1C and sew through the empty hole of the next B.

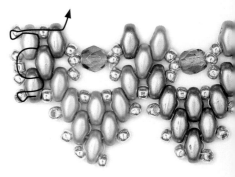

STAGE 21 To form the diamond points along the top edge of the foundation, repeat [stages 15–18 and then stages 11–14] four more times, and then stages 15–18 once again.

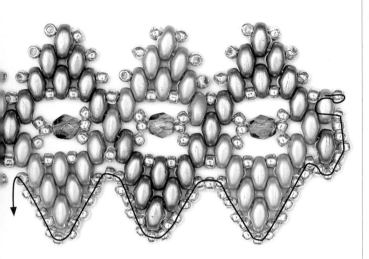

STAGE 22 You will now complete the edging of C beads all around the bracelet. Pick up 1C, turn, and sew back through the A just exited. Step up through the other hole of the same A. Sew through the 3C at the end of the foundation. Pick up 1C and sew through the next C. Pick up 3C and sew through the next C. [Pick up 1C and sew through the next C on the diamond] three times. Pick up 3C and sew through the next C. [Pick up 1C and sew through the next C] twice. Pick up 1C, skip the C in the foundation, move across to the next diamond, and sew through the next C. Continue adding 1C between the C beads along the sides of each diamond and 3C around the tip until you exit the last turn bead on the side of the last diamond at the opposite end of the bracelet.

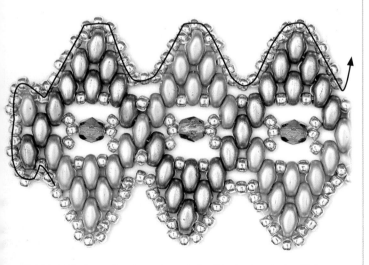

STAGE 23 Pick up 1C and sew through the C in the foundation. Pick up 3C and sew through the next C. Pick up 1C and sew through the next 3C at the end of the foundation. Pick up 1C and sew through the next C. Pick up 3C and sew through the next C. Now add C beads around the sides and tips of the diamonds, as you did in stage 22, until you exit the last turn bead on the side of the last diamond at the opposite end.

STAGE 24 Pick up 1C and sew through the C in the foundation. Pick up 3C and sew through the next C. Pick up 1C and sew through the next 2C, so that you exit the middle C at the end of the bracelet.

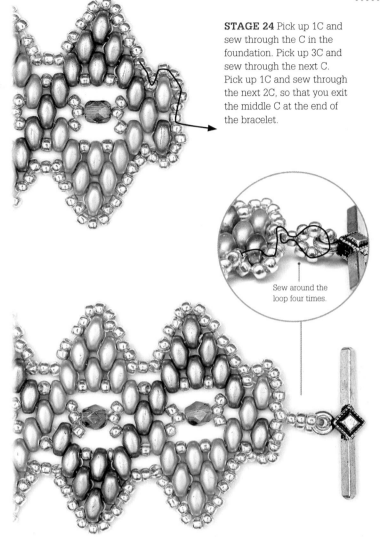

Sew around the loop four times.

STAGE 25 Pick up 4C and sew through the attachment ring on one half of the clasp. Pick up 3C and sew down through the first of the 4C and then through the middle C at the end of the bracelet (the C exited in stage 24). Sew around this loop of beads three more times for strength. Weave the remaining thread through the beads, knotting 4–5 times in between as you go, and then trim.

STAGE 26 Thread the needle with the tail of thread left at the beginning and sew through the beads to exit the middle C at the end of the bracelet. Attach the other half of the clasp in the same way as before. Weave in and fasten off the thread.

Another dimension

In this section you will learn how to add more dimension to your beadwork by using layers of beads, creating three-dimensional shapes, or cleverly using color to give the impression of layers and texture. The Savannah Necklace (page 86) also invites you to create your own colorway or pattern.

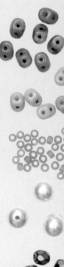

Petits Secrets Bracelet

This bracelet lives up to its name. Lift any of the little bead shells and the secret is revealed, in the shape of the pearls, and the biggest secret of all, the clasp. Where is it? It's hidden under a shell, of course. This stunning bracelet may look solid but is in fact really flexible, with lots of flow and movement.

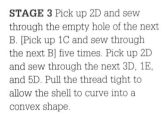

STAGE 1 Thread the needle with a comfortable length of thread; 15 in. (38cm) will complete stages 1–6. Add a stop bead, leaving a 12 in. (30cm) tail for attaching the clasp later. Pick up 1D, 1E, 1D, and 7A. Sew through all the beads again in the same direction to form a circle, and then through the first D, E, and D once more.

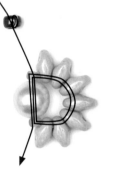

STAGE 2 Pick up 2D and sew through the empty hole of the first A. [Pick up 1B and sew through the next A] six times. Pick up 2D and sew through the next 1D, 1E, and 3D.

STAGE 3 Pick up 2D and sew through the empty hole of the next B. [Pick up 1C and sew through the next B] five times. Pick up 2D and sew through the next 3D, 1E, and 5D. Pull the thread tight to allow the shell to curve into a convex shape.

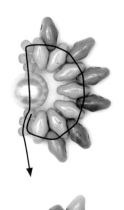

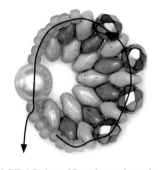

STAGE 4 Pick up 3D and sew through the empty hole of the next C. [Pick up 1F and sew through the next C] four times. Pick up 3D and sew through the next 5D, 1E, and 1D. Pull tight as you go to curve the shell. You may need to use pliers to pull the needle through. Flip the completed shell over so that the concave side is uppermost (this will be the top of the bracelet when worn).

Convex underside of shell.

Concave top of shell.

Finished length:
7 in. (18cm) including clasp

YOU WILL NEED
(beads shown actual size)

BEAD BOX
- **A** = 7g duo beads, pink
- **B** = 6g duo beads, dark green
- **C** = 5g duo beads, lime
- **D** = 4g 11° seed beads, pink
- **E** = Twenty-seven 6mm glass pearls, pink
- **F** = Fifty-six 4mm faceted crystal beads, metallic olive

HARDWARE
- 18 ft. (5.5m) thread
- 6mm or 8mm round magnetic clasp

TOOLKIT
- Size 11 or 12 beading needle
- Scissors
- Pliers
- Stop bead

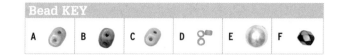

Bead KEY

A		B		C		D		E		F	

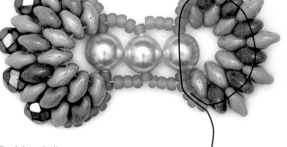

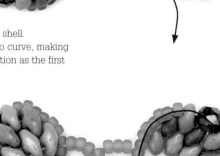

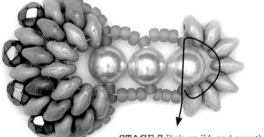

STAGE 5 You will now add a pearl link. Pick up 4D, 1E, and 4D. Sew through the middle D, E, and D of the first shell, and then through the first 4D, 1E, and 1D of this stage.

STAGE 6 You will now start adding the second shell. Pick up 4D, 1E, and 4D. Sew through the middle D, E, and D from stage 5, and then through the first 4D, 1E, and 1D of this stage.

STAGE 7 Pick up 7A and sew through middle D, E, and D from stage 6.

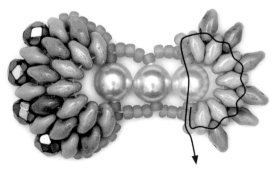

STAGE 8 Pick up 2D and sew through the empty hole of the next A. [Pick up 1B and sew through the next A] six times. Pick up 2D and sew through the next 1D, 1E, and 3D of this shell.

STAGE 9 Pick up 2D and sew through the empty hole of the next B. [Pick up 1C and sew through the next B] five times. Pick up 2D and sew through the next 3D, 1E, and 5D of this shell. Pull the thread tight to allow the shell to curve, making sure that it will curve in the same direction as the first shell once it has been flipped over.

STAGE 10 Pick up 3D and sew through the empty hole of the next C. [Pick up 1F and sew through the next C] four times. Pick up 3D and sew through the next 5D, 1E, and 1D of this shell. Pull tight as you go to curve the shell, using pliers to pull the needle through if necessary.

STAGE 11 Flip the shell over so it faces the same way as the first, with the concave side now uppermost. Repeat stages 5–10 until you have fourteen shells in total.

Follow thread path as shown on stage 13.

STAGE 12 Pick up 3D and sew through the attachment ring on one half of the clasp. Pick up 3D and sew through the middle D, E, and D of the last shell. Sew through this loop of beads twice more for strength. Weave the remaining thread through the beads, knotting 4–5 times in between as you go, and then trim.

STAGE 13 Thread the needle with the tail of thread left at the beginning. Attach the other half of the clasp in the same way as before. Weave in and fasten off the thread.

Sew around the loop three times.

Honesty Earrings

The shape of these pretty earrings is inspired by Honesty seed pods, those paper-thin white pods fluttering in the late summer breeze. Each earring is made from four faceted crystals surrounded by duo beads, with a second layer of seed beads and a smaller crystal crossing over the center, giving them a unique shape and texture.

Finished length: 1½ in. (4cm) excluding ear hook

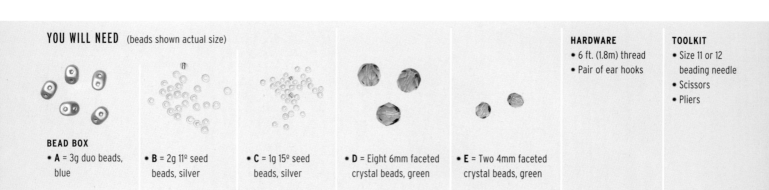

YOU WILL NEED (beads shown actual size)

BEAD BOX
• **A** = 3g duo beads, blue

• **B** = 2g 11º seed beads, silver

• **C** = 1g 15º seed beads, silver

• **D** = Eight 6mm faceted crystal beads, green

• **E** = Two 4mm faceted crystal beads, green

HARDWARE
• 6 ft. (1.8m) thread
• Pair of ear hooks

TOOLKIT
• Size 11 or 12 beading needle
• Scissors
• Pliers

See it GROW

STAGE 1 Thread the needle with 3 ft. (90cm) of thread. Pick up [1B, 1D] four times. Sew through all the beads again in the same direction to form a circle and tie a knot to secure, leaving a tail of thread to weave in later. Sew through the first B and D again and gently tug the knot inside the beads.

STAGE 2 Pick up 1B, 5A, and 1B. Sew back through the D just exited and then the next B and D from stage 1.

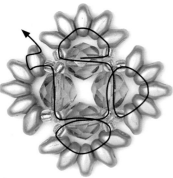

STAGE 3 Repeat stage 2 three more times, then sew through the first B and A added in stage 2. Step up by sewing back through the empty hole of the same A.

STAGE 4 [Pick up 1B and sew through the empty hole of the next A] twenty times. Weave through the next six outer beads to exit the middle A of a group of 5A; this will be the top of the earring.

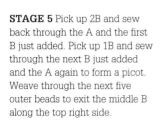

STAGE 5 Pick up 2B and sew back through the A and the first B just added. Pick up 1B and sew through the next B just added and the A again to form a picot. Weave through the next five outer beads to exit the middle B along the top right side.

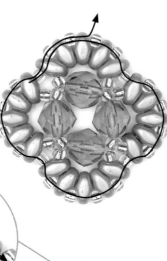

STAGE 6 Pick up 4B, 1E, and 4B. Take these beads across the earring and sew down through the B opposite the B just exited. Make sure you sew through in the right direction; you should now be working toward the bottom of the earring. Weave through the next five outer beads to exit the middle A at the bottom.

STAGE 7 Repeat stage 5 to add a picot at the bottom of the earring, but this time weave through to exit the middle B along the bottom right side.

STAGE 8 Pick up 4B and sew up through the E from stage 6. Pick up 4B and sew up through the B opposite the B just exited. Weave through the beads to exit the middle B of the top picot.

Sew around the loop three times.

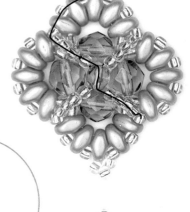

STAGE 9 Pick up 9C and sew through the B just exited to form the hanging loop. Sew around this loop of beads twice more for strength. Weave the remaining thread through the outer beads, knotting 4–5 times in between as you go, and then trim. Weave in and fasten off the beginning tail in the same way. Weave in and fasten off the beginning tail in the same way. Open the loop on the ear hook and attach the earring with the E bead at the front. Make the second earring to match.

Alicia Bracelet

Finished length:
8 in. (20cm) including clasp

Everyone loves a beaded bead, and these simple beads made with duos are no exception. Joined cleverly to create a bracelet, they can be made using from one to five colors of duos. This pattern uses three colors of duo beads, with a fourth color of seed beads. Wear the bracelet with the flatter side of the beaded beads against the skin.

YOU WILL NEED
(beads shown actual size)

BEAD BOX

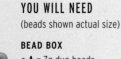

• **A** = 7g duo beads, blue

• **B** = 7g duo beads, purple

• **C** = 3g duo beads, white

• **D** = 3g 11º seed beads, green

HARDWARE
• 18½ ft. (5.6m) thread
• Toggle clasp

TOOLKIT
• Size 11 or 12 beading needle
• Scissors
• Pliers

See it GROW

STAGE 1 Stages 1–6 form the first beaded bead (see also technique below). Thread the needle with 3 ft. (90cm) of thread. This is enough for a beaded bead with clasp attachment; 2½ ft. (75cm) will be sufficient for each beaded bead without the clasp. Pick up [1D, 1A, 1D, 1B] twice. Sew through all the beads again in the same direction to form a circle and tie a knot to secure, leaving a tail of thread to weave in later. Sew through the first D and A again and gently tug the knot inside the beads. Step up by sewing back through the empty hole of the same A.

STAGE 2 *Pick up 1A, 1D, and 1B. Sew through the empty hole of the next B. Pick up 1B, 1D, and 1A. Sew through the empty hole of the next A.** Repeat from * to ** once more. Sew through the beads again to prevent them from relaxing on the thread, and finish by stepping up through the last A added.

TECHNIQUE: DIAGRAM VIEW OF THE BEADED BEAD

An open view of the beaded bead sequence.

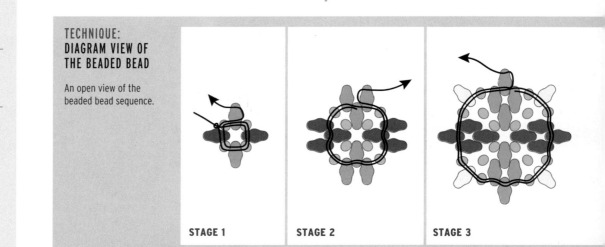

STAGE 1   STAGE 2   STAGE 3

STAGE 3 *Pick up 1D, 1C, and 1D. Sew through the empty hole of the next B. Pick up 1B and sew through the next B. Pick up 1D, 1C, and 1D. Sew through the next A. Pick up 1A and sew through the next A.** Repeat from * to ** once more. Sew through the beads again, and finish by stepping up through the last A added. You may notice the beads beginning to form a cup shape.

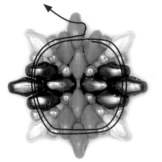

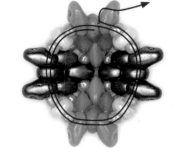

STAGE 5 *Pick up 1D and sew through the empty hole of the next B. Pick up 1B and sew through the next B. Pick up 1D and sew through the next A. Pick up 1A and sew through the next A.** Repeat from * to ** once more, pulling tight so the beads turn over to the center. Sew through the beads again, and finish by stepping up through the last A added.

STAGE 4 *Pick up 1A and 1D. Sew through the empty hole of the next C. Pick up 1D and 1B. Sew through the next B. Pick up 1B and 1D. Sew through the next C. Pick up 1D and 1A. Sew through the next A.** Repeat from * to ** once more. Sew through the beads again, and finish by stepping up through the last A added. The beads will now form a definite cup.

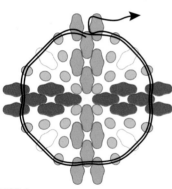

STAGE 6 *Pick up 1D and sew through the empty hole of the next B. Pick up 1D and sew through the next A.** Repeat from * to ** once more. Sew through the beads again to tighten and secure the sphere, and then weave through to exit the top hole of a C bead. Take note of the direction you weave in, because you will need to do the same on every bead to make sure they all face the same way when linked together.

Finish by exiting the top hole of a C bead.

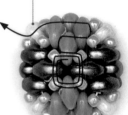

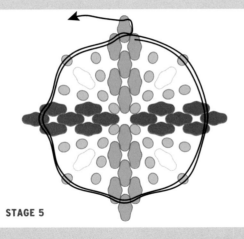
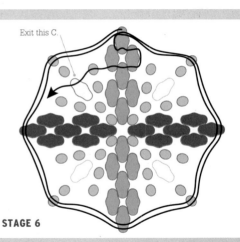

STAGE 4   **STAGE 5**   Exit this C.   **STAGE 6**

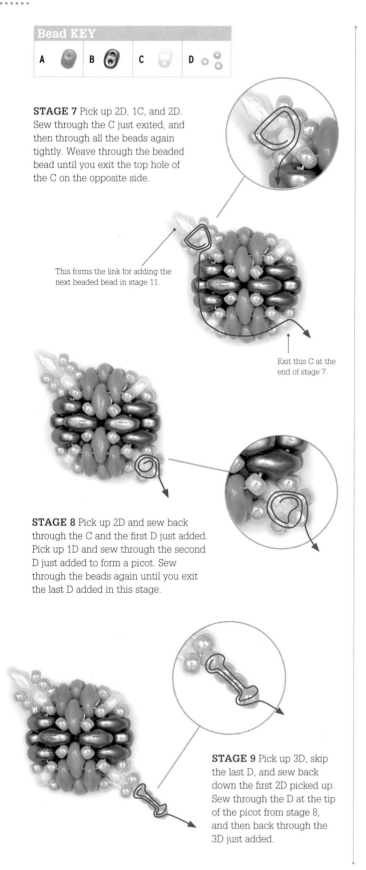

Bead KEY

A	B	C	D

STAGE 7 Pick up 2D, 1C, and 2D. Sew through the C just exited, and then through all the beads again tightly. Weave through the beaded bead until you exit the top hole of the C on the opposite side.

This forms the link for adding the next beaded bead in stage 11.

Exit this C at the end of stage 7.

STAGE 8 Pick up 2D and sew back through the C and the first D just added. Pick up 1D and sew through the second D just added to form a picot. Sew through the beads again until you exit the last D added in this stage.

STAGE 9 Pick up 3D, skip the last D, and sew back down the first 2D picked up. Sew through the D at the tip of the picot from stage 8, and then back through the 3D just added.

STAGE 10 Pick up 3D and sew through the attachment ring on one half of the clasp. Pick up 3D and sew through the last D from stage 9. Sew around this loop of beads three more times for strength, then back down the stage 9 beads. Weave the remaining thread through the beaded bead, knotting 4–5 times in between as you go, and then trim. Weave in and fasten off the beginning tail in the same way.

Sew around the loop four times.

Sew around the link four times.

STAGE 11 Repeat stages 1–6 to make the next beaded bead (see also the quick reminder opposite). Repeat stage 7 to create the next link. You will now join the new bead to the previous bead. Exiting the C opposite the link on the new bead at the end of stage 7, pick up 2D and sew through the empty hole of the C on the link of the previous bead. Pick up 2D and sew through the C just exited on the new bead. Sew through these beads three more times for strength, then weave in and fasten off the thread. Repeat this stage to make and join four more beaded beads, making six in total.

STAGE 12 Repeat stages 1–6 to make one more beaded bead (seven in total). Note that you do not repeat stage 7 to make a link this time. Exiting the C at the end of stage 6, repeat stages 8–10 to add the second half of the clasp. Weave through to the C on the opposite side of the bead and join to the previous (sixth) bead, as described in stage 11. Weave in and fasten off the thread as before.

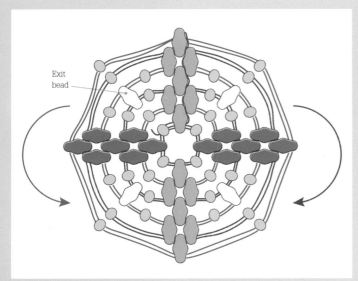

TECHNIQUE:
BEADED BEAD REMINDER

Here is an overview of the beading sequence for making a beaded bead. The threads in gray go clockwise; the threads in red go counterclockwise.

Exit
bead

Wisteria Necklace

The nodding, pendulous blooms of wisteria are reproduced using duo beads in this vibrant necklace, with the colors and freshness we expect to see at springtime. It is the perfect accessory for adding a touch of nature-inspired beauty to your look.

Finished length:
19 in. (48cm) including clasp

See it GROW

STAGE 1 Stages 1–7 form the foundation strap of the necklace. Thread the needle with a comfortable length of thread; 3 ft. (90cm) will make 12 in. (30cm) of the foundation strap. Pick up 7C and 1A. Sew through all the beads again in the same direction to form a circle and tie a knot to secure, leaving a tail of thread to weave in later. Sew through the first 4C again and gently tug the knot inside the beads.

STAGE 3 Pick up 3C and 1A. Sew through the empty hole of the A above.

Sew around the loop four times.

STAGE 2 Pick up 4C and sew through the attachment ring on one half of the clasp. Pick up 3C and sew down through the first of the 4C and then through the middle C from stage 1. Sew around this loop of beads three more times for strength. Weave through the beads from stage 1 until you exit the A.

STAGE 4 Pick up 3C and 1A. Sew through the empty hole of the A below.

STAGE 5 Pick up 3C and 1A. Sew through the empty hole of the A above.

STAGE 6 Repeat stages 4–5 another 62 times, then stage 4 once again, using 129A in total.

STAGE 7 Pick up 3C (note that you do not pick up an A this time) and sew through the empty hole of the A above. Pick up 7C and sew back through the A just exited and then the first 4C again. Attach the second half of the clasp as before (stage 2). Weave the remaining thread through the beads, knotting 4–5 times in between as you go, and then trim.

Then attach clasp as shown in stage 2.

YOU WILL NEED
(beads shown actual size)

BEAD BOX
- **A** = 9g duo beads, green
- **B** = 24g duo beads, purple
- **C** = 7g 11º seed beads, green
- **D** = 2g 15º seed beads, lilac

HARDWARE
- 30 ft. (9.1m) thread
- Toggle clasp

TOOLKIT
- Size 11 or 12 beading needle
- Scissors

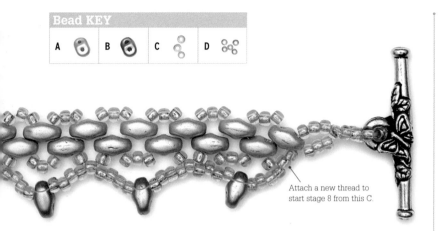

Bead KEY			
A	B	C	D

Attach a new thread to start stage 8 from this C.

STAGE 8 You will now start adding the garlands of flowers to the foundation. Attach a new thread securely, and weave through the beads until you exit the middle C from the first group of 3C added in stage 7, working toward the center of the necklace. *Pick up 4C, 1B, and 4C. Skip the next group of 3C in the foundation, and sew through the middle C of the next group of 3C.** Repeat from * to ** all the way to the other end of the foundation, using 32B in total.

STAGE 9 Weave through the beads at the end of the foundation and turn to work back toward the center of the necklace, taking care that the thread does not show while turning. Continue until you exit the last B added, and then step up by sewing back through the empty hole of the same B.

STAGE 10 You will now complete one flower at a time all along the necklace. Pick up 1B and 1D. Turn and sew back through the B just added and then the B just exited.

D beads are used as "turn" beads for sewing back and forth to create the flowers.

STAGE 11 Pick up 1B and 1D. Turn and sew back through the B just added, the B just exited, and the B and D from stage 10.

STAGE 12 Pick up 2D and sew through the empty hole of the B. Pick up 3B and sew through the empty hole of the next B (from stage 11). Pick up 1D, turn, and sew back through 2B. Step up through the B just exited.

STAGE 13 Pick up 1D, turn, and sew back through the B. [Pick up 1B and sew through the next B] twice. Pick up 1D, turn, and sew back through 2B. Step up through the B just exited.

STAGE 14 Pick up 1D, turn, and sew through the B. Pick up 2B and sew through the empty hole of the next B. Pick up 1D, turn, and sew back through 2B. Step up through the B just exited.

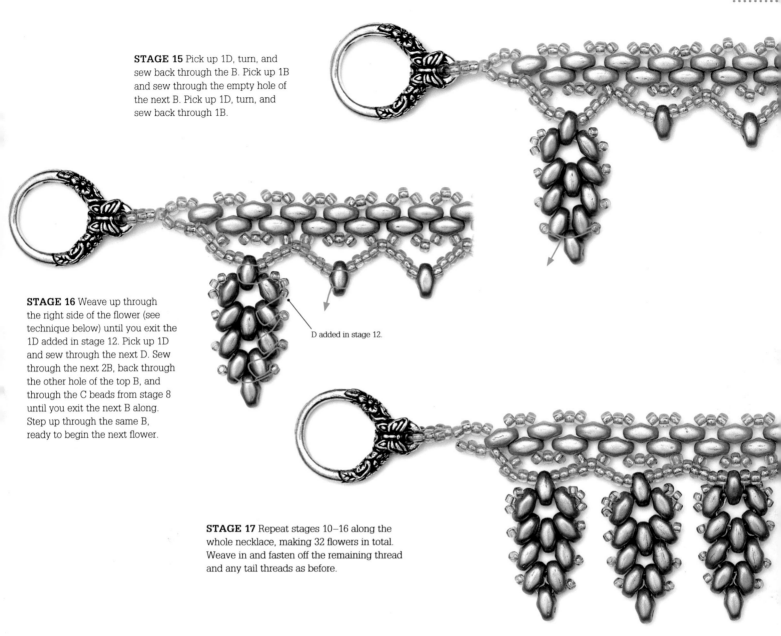

STAGE 15 Pick up 1D, turn, and sew back through the B. Pick up 1B and sew through the empty hole of the next B. Pick up 1D, turn, and sew back through 1B.

STAGE 16 Weave up through the right side of the flower (see technique below) until you exit the 1D added in stage 12. Pick up 1D and sew through the next D. Sew through the next 2B, back through the other hole of the top B, and through the C beads from stage 8 until you exit the next B along. Step up through the same B, ready to begin the next flower.

D added in stage 12.

STAGE 17 Repeat stages 10–16 along the whole necklace, making 32 flowers in total. Weave in and fasten off the remaining thread and any tail threads as before.

TECHNIQUE: WEAVING BACK UP THROUGH THE FLOWERS (STAGE 16)

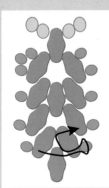

STEP 1
Sew through the next 2B and 1D. Turn and sew back through 1B. Step up through the same B.

STEP 2
Sew through the next 1B and 1D. Turn and sew back through 1B. Step up through the same B.

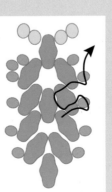

STEP 3
Sew through the next 1B and 1D. Turn and sew back through 1B. Step up through the same B. Sew through the next 1B and 1D, then continue as described in stage 16.

Sparkling Swags Necklace

Crystal accents add eye-catching sparkle to this stunning necklace with an echo of Deco. The duo bead shells rest smoothly against the breastbone with a delicate flow like lace, with the cascading swags holding them all together.

Finished length:
19 in. (48cm) including clasp

STAGE 1 Stages 1–7 form the foundation strap of the necklace. Thread the needle with a comfortable length of thread; 3 ft. (90cm) will make 12 in. (30cm) of the foundation strap. Pick up 7B and 1A. Sew through all the beads again in the same direction to form a circle and tie a knot to secure, leaving a tail of thread to weave in later. Sew through the first 4B again and gently tug the knot inside the beads.

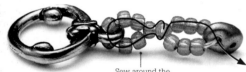

Sew around the loop four times.

STAGE 2 Pick up 4B and sew through the attachment ring on one half of the clasp. Pick up 3B and sew down through the first of the 4B and then through the middle B from stage 1. Sew around this loop of beads three more times for strength. Weave through the beads from stage 1 until you exit the A.

STAGE 5 Pick up 3B and 1A. Sew through the empty hole of the A above.

STAGE 6 Repeat stages 4–5 another 63 times, then stage 4 once again, using 131A in total.

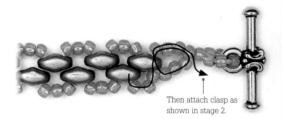

Then attach clasp as shown in stage 2.

STAGE 7 Pick up 3B (note that you do not pick up an A this time) and sew through the empty hole of the A above. Pick up 7B and sew back through the A just exited and then the first 4B again. Attach the second half of the clasp as before (stage 2). Weave the remaining thread through the beads, knotting 4–5 times in between as you go, and then trim.

YOU WILL NEED

(beads shown actual size)

BEAD BOX
- **A** = 15g duo beads, gold

- **B** = 14g 11° seed beads, blue

- **C** = Forty-two 4mm crystal bicones, gold

HARDWARE
- 42 ft. (12.8m) thread
- Toggle clasp

TOOLKIT
- Size 11 or 12 beading needle
- Scissors
- Pliers
- Four 8mm jump rings (used as markers)

STAGE 3 Pick up 3B and 1A. Sew through the empty hole of the A above.

STAGE 4 Pick up 3B and 1A. Sew through the empty hole of the A below.

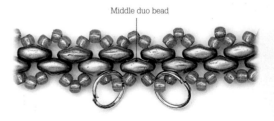

Middle duo bead

STAGE 8 Now you need to mark some of the beads with jump rings. Locate the middle A bead in the lower row. Place a jump ring around the group of 3B on each side of the middle A. Next count 18 groups of 3B from the jump ring marker on one side. Place a jump ring around the 18th group of 3B. Do the same on the other side.

Bead KEY

A	B	C
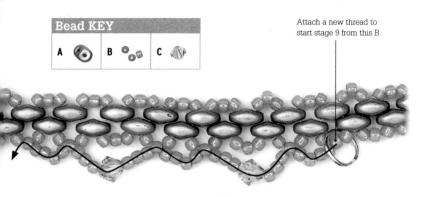		

A (round bead), B (seed beads), C (crystal)

Attach a new thread to start stage 9 from this B.

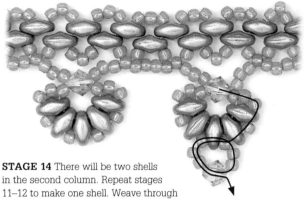

STAGE 13 Weave through the beads of the foundation to move the thread to the position of the next column of shells, exiting the next C along (see technique below).

STAGE 9 Attach a new thread securely to the right-hand side of the necklace, weaving through the beads until you exit the middle B of the group of 3B marked by the jump ring, working toward the middle of the necklace. You will now add the first row of crystals that form the base of each shell. *Pick up 4B and sew through the middle B of the next group of 3B. Pick up 3B, 1C, and 3B. Skip the next group of 3B and sew through the middle B of the next group of 3B.** Repeat from * to ** eleven times. Pick up 4B and sew through the middle B marked by the jump ring at the left-hand side of the necklace.

STAGE 10 Turn and weave through the beads until you exit the first C, working from the left-hand jump ring toward the middle of the necklace (see technique below). You can remove the markers now.

STAGE 14 There will be two shells in the second column. Repeat stages 11–12 to make one shell. Weave through the beads around the right-hand side of the shell until you exit the middle B, A, and B at the bottom of the shell. Pick up 2B, 1C, and 2B. Sew through the middle B, A, and B of the shell again, and then through the first 2B and 1C just added.

STAGE 15 Repeat stages 11–12 to make the second shell in this column, exiting the C to finish.

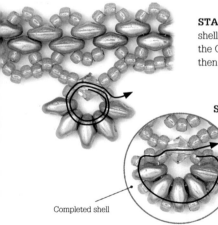

STAGE 11 You will now start forming the first shell. Pick up 1B, 5A, and 1B. Sew back through the C. Sew through all the beads once more and then through the first B just added.

STAGE 12 Pick up 2B and sew through the empty hole of the first A of the shell. [Pick up 1B and sew through the next A] four times. Pick up 2B and sew through the next B and C to complete the shell.

Completed shell

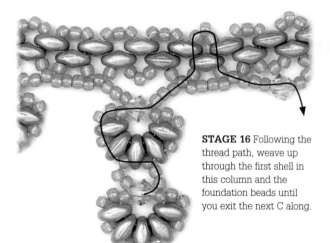

STAGE 16 Following the thread path, weave up through the first shell in this column and the foundation beads until you exit the next C along.

TECHNIQUE: TURNING AND WEAVING THROUGH THE SHELLS AND SWAGS

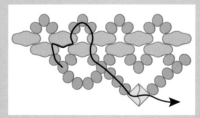

TURNING TO START THE FIRST SHELL (STAGE 10)
Sew up through the next B in the group of 3B marked by the jump ring and then through the A in the lower row of duo beads in the foundation. Take the thread across the next A to sew up through the other hole. Sew through the next 3B, down through the next 2A and 2B of the foundation, and then through the next 3B and 1C from stage 9.

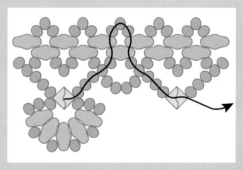

MOVING TO NEXT COLUMN OF SHELLS (STAGE 13)
When one column of shells is complete, weave up through the shells, following the thread path. After exiting the C of the top shell, sew up through the next 3B from stage 9, through 2B from the next group of 3B, and then through 2A and 3B of the foundation. Sew down through the next 2A and 2B of the foundation, and then through the next 3B and 1C from stage 9.

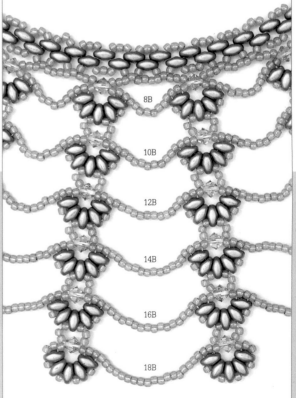

STAGE 17 Add four more columns of shells, increasing the number of shells by one in each column, until the last column at the middle of the necklace is six shells long. Add six more columns along the second half of the necklace, decreasing the number of shells in each by one shell. Weave in and fasten off the remaining thread.

STAGE 18 Attach a new thread at the left-hand side of the necklace, and weave through the beads until you exit the C at the top of the first shell, working toward the middle of the necklace.

STAGE 19 Now add a row of swags connecting the top row of shells. Sew through the next 3B across the top of the first shell. *Pick up 8B and sew through the 3B, 1C, and 3B across the top of the next shell along.** Repeat from * to ** ten more times to complete the first row of swags.

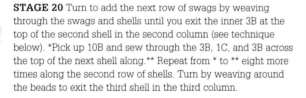

STAGE 20 Turn to add the next row of swags by weaving through the swags and shells until you exit the inner 3B at the top of the second shell in the second column (see technique below). *Pick up 10B and sew through the 3B, 1C, and 3B across the top of the next shell along.** Repeat from * to ** eight more times along the second row of shells. Turn by weaving around the beads to exit the third shell in the third column.

STAGE 21 Repeat the process of adding swags across each row of shells, increasing the number of B beads by two on each row, until there are 18 beads between the bottom two shells of the six-shell columns at the middle of the necklace. Weave in and fasten off the remaining thread and any tail threads.

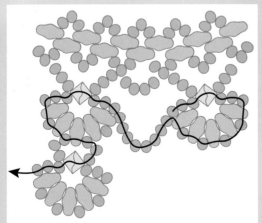

TURNING FOR NEXT ROW OF SWAGS (STAGE 20)
When adding the last swag in a row, you will finish by sewing through the 3B, 1C, and 3B across the top of the last shell. Continue to weave through the beads around the bottom of the shell and then back through the last swag. Sew through the 3B, 1C, and 3B across the top of the next shell, and then through the next six beads (3A and 3B) around the bottom of the shell. Sew down through the next 2B to the shell below, then through 1C and 3B at the top of the shell, ready to add the next row of swags.

Savannah Necklace

Color can change the mood, look, and feel of a piece, even when the pattern is identical. This necklace is made in three parts: the central diamond, the side panels, and finally the neck straps. The central diamond can be made in any design and in as many colors as you wish; use the template provided to experiment with different color combinations and patterns (see also page 26).

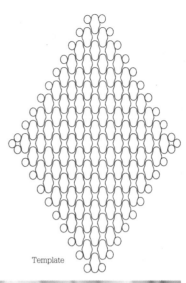

Template

Finished length: 18 in. (46cm) including clasp

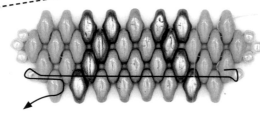

See it GROW

STAGE 1 Stages 1–9 form the central diamond. Cut 6 ft. (1.8m) of thread and place a needle on each end. Pick up 3E and slide them down to the middle of the thread. With the first needle, pick up 19 duo beads in the correct color sequence for your pattern. To match the design shown, you will need 5A, 3B, 3D, 3B, and 5A. Then pick up another 3E and place the first needle to one side.

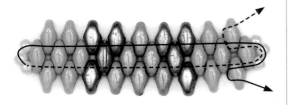

STAGE 2 With the second needle, sew through the empty hole of the first A picked up. You will now sew through the empty holes of alternate duo beads, adding one duo bead between them in the following sequence: 2A, 1B, 3D, 1B, 2A. Exiting the last A, sew through the next 3E and back through 2A. Step up by sewing back through the empty hole of the A just exited. With the first needle, sew through 2A and step up through the A just exited. Now continue with the first needle only to form the lower half of the diamond.

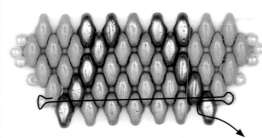

STAGE 3 E beads are now used as "turn" beads for sewing back and forth across the duo beads. Pick up 1E, turn, and sew back through the A just exited. Working across the row in pattern, add 1A, 1B, 4D, 1B, 1A, and 1E to turn. Sew back through 2A and then step up through the A just exited.

STAGE 4 Pick up 1E to turn, then across the row add 1B, 5D, 1B, and 1E to turn. Step up through the last B added.

STAGE 5 Continue in this way to add five more rows of D beads, starting with 6D on the first of these rows and reducing the number of beads by one on each row, to end with 2D on the fifth. Use 1E to turn at the end of each row.

STAGE 6 Pick up 1E to turn and sew back through the D just exited. Pick up 1D and sew through the next D. Pick up 1E to turn, then sew back through 2D and step up through the last D added. Add 1E on each side of the last D. Weave the remaining thread through the beads, knotting 4–5 times in between as you go, and then trim.

Stage 5

Stage 6

STAGE 7 Now use the second needle to form the upper half of the diamond. Pick up 1E, turn, and sew back through the first A. Working across the row, add 1A, 1B, 1C, 2B, 1C, 1B, 1A, and 1E to turn. Sew back through 2A and then step up through the A just exited.

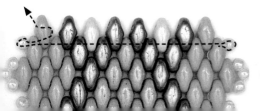

STAGE 8 Pick up 1E to turn, then across the row add 1B, 2C, 1B, 2C, 1B, and 1E to turn. Step up through the last C added.

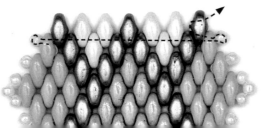

STAGE 9 Repeat stages 5–6 using C instead of D, then fasten off the thread. Now start the right-hand side panel by attaching a new thread—6 ft. (1.8m) will complete the panel—and weaving through to exit the E bead indicated.

Exit this E to start the side panel.

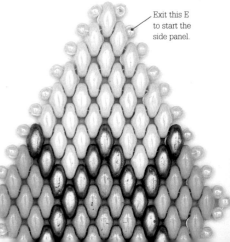

YOU WILL NEED
(beads shown actual size)

BEAD BOX
- **A** = 3g duo beads, beige
- **B** = 14g duo beads, gold
- **C** = 3g duo beads, cream
- **D** = 10g duo beads, pink
- **E** = 11g 11º seed beads, cream
- **F** = Thirty-two 4mm faceted crystal beads, dark pink

HARDWARE
- 42 ft. (12.8m) thread
- Four-ring slider clasp

TOOLKIT
- Two size 11 or 12 beading needles
- Scissors

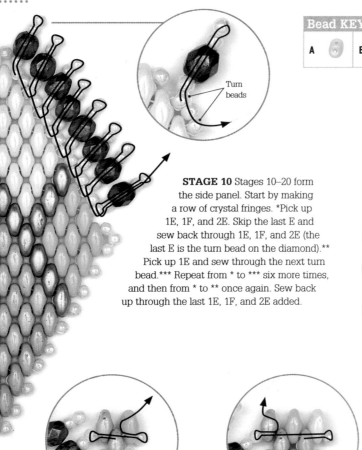

Turn beads

Bead KEY

A	B	C	D	E	F

STAGE 10 Stages 10–20 form the side panel. Start by making a row of crystal fringes. *Pick up 1E, 1F, and 2E. Skip the last E and sew back through 1E, 1F, and 2E (the last E is the turn bead on the diamond).** Pick up 1E and sew through the next turn bead.*** Repeat from * to *** six more times, and then from * to ** once again. Sew back up through the last 1E, 1F, and 2E added.

STAGE 11 You will now add a panel of duo beads in a diagonal four-row striped color sequence. Pick up 1D and 1E to turn. Sew back through the D, turn through the E at the end of the crystal fringe, sew back through the D, and then step up through the D.

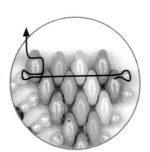

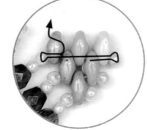

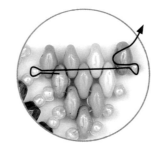

STAGE 12 Pick up 1D, turn through the E at the end of the next crystal fringe, and sew back through the D just added and the next D. Pick up 1A and 1E to turn. Sew back through the A and step up, keeping the beads tight.

STAGE 13 Pick up 1C and 1E to turn. Sew back through the C and the next A. Pick up 1A and sew through the next D. Pick up 1D and turn through the E at the end of the next crystal fringe. Sew back through the last D and step up.

STAGE 14 Pick up 1D and turn through the E at the end of the next crystal fringe. Sew back through 2D. Pick up 1A and sew through the next A. Pick up 1C and sew through the next C. Pick up 1D and 1E to turn. Sew back through the D and step up.

STAGE 15 Pick up 1E to turn and sew back through the D. Add 1D, 1C, 1A, and 1D across the row. Turn through the E at the end of the next fringe. Sew back through the last D and step up.

STAGE 16 Continue adding duo beads in this way, maintaining the color sequence, until you have attached beads to all of the crystal fringes. At this point, you should be exiting an outer D after stepping up. Next, pick up 1E to turn and sew back through the D. Add 1D, 1C, and 1A across the row. Sew through the last D and pick up 1E to turn. Sew back through the D and A, and step up through the A.

STAGE 17 Continue adding the correct color duo beads across the rows and turn beads at each end. Finish by exiting the turn bead at the top right.

STAGE 18 Repeat stage 10 to add another row of crystal fringes, but this time using 2E, 1F, and 3E for each fringe.

STAGE 19 Now add another panel of duo beads (see stages 11–17), but this time with five diagonal rows of beads. This sample uses D beads throughout, but you could create another striped pattern if you prefer. Finish by exiting the turn bead at the top right.

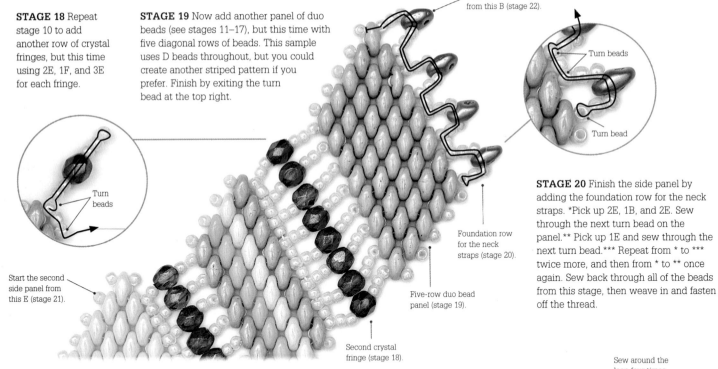

Start the neck straps from this B (stage 22).

Turn beads

Turn bead

Foundation row for the neck straps (stage 20).

Five-row duo bead panel (stage 19).

Second crystal fringe (stage 18).

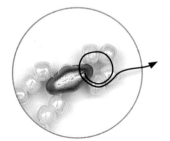

Turn beads

Start the second side panel from this E (stage 21).

STAGE 20 Finish the side panel by adding the foundation row for the neck straps. *Pick up 2E, 1B, and 2E. Sew through the next turn bead on the panel.** Pick up 1E and sew through the next turn bead.*** Repeat from * to *** twice more, and then from * to ** once again. Sew back through all of the beads from this stage, then weave in and fasten off the thread.

STAGE 21 Attach a new thread to the top left of the central diamond and repeat stages 10–20 to add the second side panel.

STAGE 22 Stages 22–26 form the neck straps. Attach a new thread—3 ft. (90cm) will be enough for each strap—and weave through the beads until you exit the B at the top of the foundation row of 4B on one of the side panels. Step up through the empty hole of this B. Pick up 4E and sew back through the B and the first 2E just added to form a circle.

STAGE 23 Pick up 1B and sew through the circle of beads from stage 22 and the B just added. Step up through the empty hole of this B. Continue in this way until there are 22B in the strap, including the B from the foundation row. Finish by stepping up through the final B.

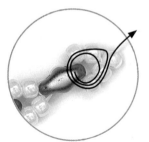

STAGE 24 Pick up 4E and sew through back through the B and the first 2E just added. Pick up 1E and sew through the next 2E just added to form a picot. Sew through the beads again to exit the last E added at the tip of the picot.

Sew around the loop four times.

STAGE 25 Pick up 4E and sew through the top loop of the slider clasp, taking care not to twist the strap. Pick up 3E and sew down through the first of the 4E and then through the E at the tip of the picot on the strap. Sew around this loop of beads three more times for strength. Weave in and fasten off the thread.

Strap 1 = 22B
Strap 2 = 23B
Strap 3 = 24B
Strap 4 = 25B

STAGE 26 Repeat stages 22–25 to attach three more straps to the same side of the clasp, adding one extra B bead to the length of each strap. So strap 1 (innermost strap when worn) has 22B, strap 2 has 23B, strap 3 has 24B, and strap 4 has 25B. This allows for the curve around the neck. Be careful not to twist the straps together, and make sure all the beads are laying the same way. Add four matching straps to the other side of the necklace, attaching them to the loops on the other side of the clasp and fastening off all threads securely.

Dazzling with crystals

These projects give you the opportunity to play with sparkling crystal rivolis, which can be showcased beautifully within a beaded bezel. You will learn how to embellish them with duos and other beads to create wonderfully dazzling jewelry that can be worn any time, day or evening.

Crystal Bloom Bracelet

This bracelet is not as tricky as it looks. The gorgeous crystal rivolis are held securely within a little pocket of seed beads, with duo beads cleverly fanning out around them like petals. Each flower component is made separately and then joined onto the previous one before fastening off. The faceted crystal beads in the links add sparkle and zest.

YOU WILL NEED
(beads shown actual size)

BEAD BOX
- **A** = 8g duo beads, blue
- **B** = 2g 11º seed beads, gold
- **C** = Six 6mm faceted crystal beads, gold
- **D** = Five 12mm crystal rivolis, gold

HARDWARE
- 15 ft. (4.5m) thread
- Toggle clasp

TOOLKIT
- Size 11 or 12 beading needle
- Scissors

Finished length:
7½ in. (19cm) including clasp

Bead KEY

A	B	C	D

See it GROW

STAGE 1 Stages 1–5 secure the crystal rivoli into the beadwork (see also technique below). Thread the needle with 3 ft. (90cm) of thread. Pick up [1B, 2A] eight times. Sew through all the beads again in the same direction to form a circle and tie a knot to secure, leaving a tail of thread to weave in later. Sew through the first B again and gently tug the knot inside the beads.

STAGE 4 *Pick up 1B and sew back through the B just exited. Sew through the next 2A and 1B from stage 1.** Repeat from * to ** seven more times. Sew back through the first B added in this stage.

Sew around the circle of B beads three more times to secure the rivoli.

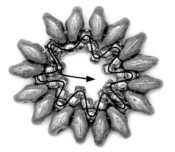

STAGE 5 *Pick up 2B and sew through the next B from stage 4.** Repeat from * to ** seven more times. Sew through the first 2B added in this stage and the next B from stage 4. Place a rivoli (D) into the center, with the front of the crystal uppermost, and pull the beads tight to cinch them together and hold the rivoli in place. Sew through the circle of B beads three more times for strength.

REVERSE SIDE

STAGE 2 *Pick up 3B, skip the next 2A, and sew through the next B.** Repeat from * to ** seven more times. Sew through the first 2B added in this stage.

STAGE 3 *Pick up 1B and sew through the middle B of the next group of 3B from stage 2.** Repeat from * to ** seven more times, pulling the thread tight to cinch the beads together. Weave through the beads until you exit a B from stage 1.

STAGE 6 Stages 6–10 complete the flower unit. Sew back through the next 1B and 1A from stage 1. Step up by sewing back through the empty hole of the same A.

TECHNIQUE: DIAGRAM VIEW OF SECURING THE CRYSTAL RIVOLI

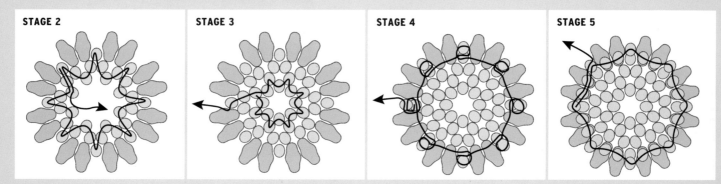

STAGE 2　　　**STAGE 3**　　　**STAGE 4**　　　**STAGE 5**

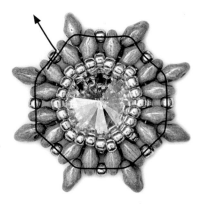

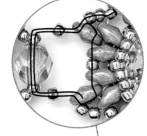

STAGE 7 *Pick up 1B and sew through the empty hole of the next A. Pick up 1A and sew through the next A.** Repeat from * to ** seven more times. Sew through the first B again.

STAGE 11 Repeat stages 1–10 to make the next flower, but do not add a second crystal to this flower. So instead of picking up 2B, 1C, and 2B at the beginning of the final repeat of stage 9, this time pick up 1B and sew through the middle B, C, and B on the side of the previous flower, then pick up 1B. Complete the flower as before.

STAGE 8 *Pick up 2B and sew through the empty hole of the next A. Pick up 2B and sew through the next B from stage 7.** Repeat from * to ** once more. Pick up 2B and sew through the empty hole of the next A.

Exit this B after adding the last flower in stage 12.

STAGE 12 Repeat stage 11 to add three more flowers, but don't fasten off the thread at the end of the last flower. This time, weave through the outer beads around the top of the flower until you exit the B below the C on the right-hand side.

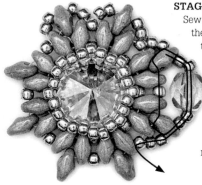

STAGE 9 Pick up 2B, 1C, and 2B. Sew through the empty hole of the next A, then back through the other hole of the same A. Sew across the next 1A, 1B, and 2A. Sew back through the other hole of the A just exited, and then through the next 2B, 1C, 2B, and 1A. Pick up 2B and sew through the next B from stage 7.

STAGE 13 Pick up 9B and sew through the middle B, C, and B on the side of the flower. Sew through these beads once more, and then through the first 5B again.

Sew around the loop four times.

STAGE 14 Pick up 4B and sew through the attachment ring on one half of the clasp. Pick up 3B and sew down through the first of the 4B and then back through the middle B at the end of the bracelet. Sew around this loop of beads three more times for strength. Weave through the beads to the flower motif.

STAGE 10 Repeat stages 8–9 once more to complete the flower. Weave the remaining thread through the beads, knotting 4–5 times in between as you go, and then trim. Weave in and fasten off the beginning tail in the same way.

STAGE 15 Weave through the length of the bracelet to the other end (or fasten off and attach a new thread if you prefer). Attach the other half of the clasp in the same way. Weave in and fasten off any thread tails.

Triskele Pendant

Celtic knotwork is a hugely popular art form, and can look stunning when incorporated into beadwork jewelry designs. This pendant, based on the well-known triskele pattern of three interlocked spirals, features a double triskele in contrasting colors surrounding a sparkling crystal rivoli.

YOU WILL NEED
(beads shown actual size)

BEAD BOX

• **A** = 3g duo beads, green

• **B** = 3g duo beads, gold

• **C** = 1g 11º cylinder beads, green

• **D** = 1g 15º seed beads, gold

• **E** = 1g 15º seed beads, green

• **F** = 1g 11º seed beads, gold

• **G** = 1g 11º seed beads, green

• **H** = One 14mm crystal rivoli, green

HARDWARE
• 8 ft. (2.4m) thread
• Cord, ribbon, or chain with clasp

TOOLKIT
• Size 10 or 11 beading needle
• Scissors
• Pliers

Finished diameter:
2 in. (5cm) excluding bail

Tip Adapting the size of bezel

For future projects that you might like to design for yourself, here is a table showing how many C beads you will need for the stage 1 circle for different sizes of rivolis. For larger rivolis, you may also be more comfortable adding an extra row of C beads to the bezel.

Rivoli	Stage 1 circle
12mm	32C
14mm	36C
16mm	42C
18mm	46C

 See it GROW

STAGE 1 Stages 1–6 use the peyote stitch beadwork technique to form the bezel that holds the rivoli (see also technique panel below). Thread the needle with 3 ft. (90cm) of thread and pick up 36C. Sew through all the beads again in the same direction to form a circle, leaving a tail of thread to weave in later. Sew through the first C again.

Beads are placed in the gaps on subsequent rows of peyote stitch.

STAGE 2 *Pick up 1C, skip the next C in the circle, and sew through the next C.** This forms peyote stitch. Repeat from * to ** all the way around the circle. Step up by sewing through the first C added in this stage.

STAGE 3 Peyote stitch around the circle again, but this time add a row of D beads. Step up through the first D added. Pull tight to cinch the beads together. The beads will now form a small tube.

You will weave through to exit a C on the bottom row at the end of stage 4.

STAGE 4 Peyote stitch around the circle again using D beads. Step up through the first bead added in this stage, pulling tight to cinch the beads together. Weave through the beads to exit a C bead on the bottom row of the bezel.

REVERSE SIDE

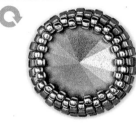

STAGE 5 Place the rivoli (H) into the bezel, with the back of the rivoli facing toward the D beads just added.

STAGE 6 Now working on the front of the bezel, peyote stitch two more rows of D beads. Again, pull tight to cinch the beads together. Fasten off the thread and attach a new 5 ft. (1.5m) length to continue. Weave through the beads to exit a C bead on the top row of C beads on the front of the bezel.

Exit a bead on the top row of C beads at the end of stage 6.

TECHNIQUE: DIAGRAM VIEW OF THE PEYOTE STITCH BEZEL

Note that stages 2–4 show the back of the bezel; stage 6 shows the front.

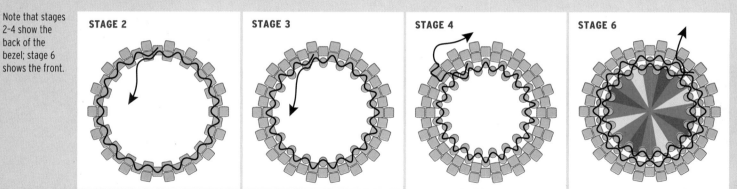

STAGE 2   STAGE 3   STAGE 4   STAGE 6

Bead KEY

A	B	C	D	E	F	G

C beads at the front of the bezel.

Front foundation beads added.

C beads at the back of the bezel.

Back foundation beads added.

STAGE 7 Peyote stitch one row of C beads on top of the C beads at the front of the bezel. Turn the bezel over and peyote stitch one row of C beads on top of the C beads at the back of the bezel. Turn the bezel over again and step up through the first C added in this stage. The two peyote stitch rows added in this stage form the foundation beads for the triskele design. They are equal to each other and are referred to as "front" and "back" foundation beads in the instructions that follow. You should have exited a front foundation bead.

Dashed lines indicate the thread path weaving through the foundation beads of the bezel.

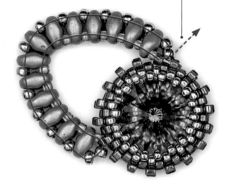

STAGE 8 *Pick up [1E, 1A] five times, 1E, 3A, 1E, and [1A, 1E] five times. Count six foundation beads counterclockwise around the bezel, and sew through the back foundation bead. Pick up 2G and sew through the empty hole of the first A. [Pick up 1G and sew through the next A] twelve times. Pick up 2G and sew through the front foundation bead from which the loop started.** Weave across the bezel until you exit the equivalent back foundation bead, sewing away from the loop.

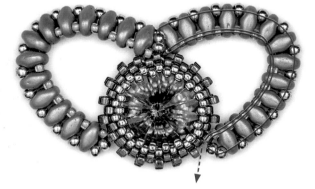

STAGE 9 Repeat stage 8 from * to ** to add another loop, but this time you are starting from a back foundation bead and should count six beads clockwise around the bezel to join the loop to a front foundation bead. Sew back through all the inner beads of the loop, then weave across the bezel until you exit the back foundation bead, sewing away from the loop.

First loop

Second loop

STAGE 10 Repeat stage 9 to add one more loop, but instead of sewing back through the inner beads of the loop at the end, this time weave counterclockwise through the bezel to exit the third front foundation bead along.

STAGE 11 Repeat stage 8 using gold duos and seed beads (B, D, and F). Note that you are taking the gold loop over and then behind the green loops.

STAGE 12 Repeat stage 9 to add a second gold loop. This time, take the gold loop behind and then over the green loops.

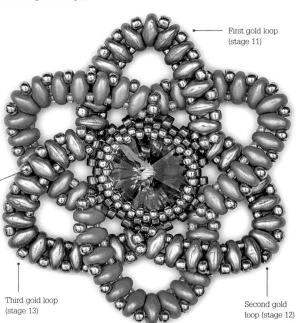

First gold loop (stage 11)

Exit this F at the end of stage 13.

Third gold loop (stage 13)

Second gold loop (stage 12)

STAGE 13 Repeat stage 9 to add a third gold loop, again taking the gold loop behind and then over the green loops. After sewing back through the inner beads of this loop, continue to weave through the first eight outer beads of the same loop until you exit the F bead indicated above.

STAGE 14 The loops will be very floppy at this stage, so you will now add a seed bead between the loops to stabilize them. Pick up 1F and sew through the G equal in place on the next loop. Sew back through the F just added and the F on the first loop. Sew once again through the F just added and the G on the next loop. Continue sewing through the outer beads of this loop until you reach the equivalent bead on the other side. Join the two loops together in the same way, using the color of the front loop for the single added bead. Repeat all the way around until all the loops are joined, then sew through the outer beads until you reach the top B of a gold loop.

Match the joining bead to the color of the front loop.

STAGE 15 You will now make a simple seed bead bail. Exiting the B at the top of a gold loop, pick up 2F and sew back through the B and the first F just added.

STAGE 16 Pick up 2F and sew back through the second F from stage 15, the B at the top of the pendant, the first F from stage 15, and the first F just added.

STAGE 17 *Pick up 2F and sew down through the second F from stage 16, up through the first F from stage 16, and up through the first F just added.** Repeat from * to ** until the bail is long enough to bend back on itself to form a loop (16–20 pairs of beads should be enough).

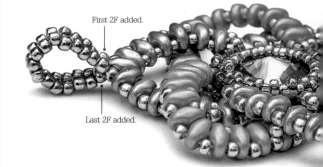

First 2F added.

Last 2F added.

STAGE 18 Sew through the F from stage 15, the B at the top of the pendant, and the other F from in stage 15. Sew around these beads and the last 2F from stage 17 three more times for strength. Weave the remaining thread through the beads, knotting 4–5 times in between as you go, and then trim. Weave in and fasten off the beginning tail in the same way.

REVERSE SIDE

Corona Pendant

Instead of using duo beads as the main feature, this pendant demonstrates how they can be used as embellishments to great effect. They give a textured appearance to the whole piece, lifting the layers and shape of the flower. Resembling a daffodil or waterlily, the combination of colors that can be used for this pendant is endless.

Finished diameter:
2¼ in. (4.5cm) excluding hanging loop

Exit a bead on the top row of C beads at the end of stage 6.

Exit a bead on the center row of C beads at the end of stage 7.

STAGES 1–6 Thread the needle with 3 ft. (90cm) of thread. Following stages 1–6 on page 95, make a peyote stitch bezel around the crystal rivoli (E) using C and D beads. Fasten off the thread and attach a new 4 ft. (1.2m) length to continue. Weave through the beads to exit a C bead on the top row of C beads on the front of the bezel at the end of stage 6.

STAGE 7 Peyote stitch one row of C beads on top of the C beads at the front of the bezel. Weave through the beads to exit a C in the center row of C beads on the side of the bezel. You will be working only from this row for the petals.

Top row of C beads added in stage 7.

The petals will be attached to this center row of C beads.

YOU WILL NEED (beads shown actual size)

BEAD BOX
• **A** = 3g duo beads, navy

• **B** = 4g 11º cylinder beads, light blue

• **C** = 1g 11º cylinder beads, white

• **D** = 2g 15º seed beads, dark blue

• **E** = One 14mm crystal rivoli, crystal AB

HARDWARE
• 10 ft. (3m) thread
• Bail
• Cord, ribbon, or chain with clasp

TOOLKIT
• Size 11 or 12 beading needle
• Scissors
• Pliers

Dashed lines indicate thread going through beads below.

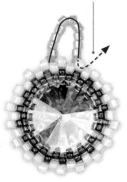

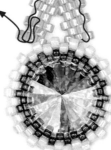

STAGE 11 Peyote stitch 4B up the right side, add 2B between the 2B at the tip, and peyote stitch 4B down the left side. Make a turn as described in the technique panel below.

STAGE 8 Stages 8–13 form the first peyote stitch petal. Pick up 12B. Working clockwise, skip the next C in the center row of the bezel and sew through the next C.

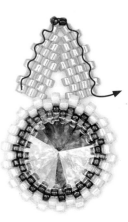

STAGE 9 Now start working in peyote stitch. Pick up 1B, skip the last B added in stage 8, and sew through the next B. [Pick up 1B, skip the next B, and sew through the next B] twice. Pick up 2B and sew through the next B. [Pick up 1B, skip the next B, and sew through the next B] twice. Pick up 1B and turn as described in the technique panel below to anchor this bead.

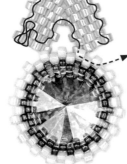

STAGE 12 Peyote stitch 4B up the left side, add 2D between the 2B at the tip, and peyote stitch 4B down the right side.

STAGE 13 Peyote stitch 5B up the right side, add 1D between the 2D at the tip, and peyote stitch 5B down the left side. Make a turn to anchor the last bead as before, and then weave through the inner beads of the petal to the other side. Sew through the C bead on the bezel where the right side of the petal is attached. Working clockwise, weave through the bezel to exit the next C along.

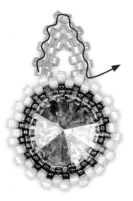

STAGE 10 Continue using peyote stitch to complete the petals. For the next row, peyote stitch 3B up the left side, add 2B between the 2B at the tip of the petal, and peyote stitch 3B down the right side. Note that the final bead picked up does not need a special turn to anchor it on the right-hand side of the petal.

STAGE 14 Repeat stages 8–13 five more times around the rivoli bezel to make six peyote petals in total. The petals will overlap at this stage. When you have completed the last petal, fasten off the thread instead of weaving back through to the bezel. Attach a new 3 ft. (90cm) length of thread and weave through the beads to exit up through the B at the bottom left-hand corner of a petal.

TECHNIQUE: TURNING AT THE END OF A ROW ON THE LEFT-HAND SIDE (STAGES 9, 11, 13)

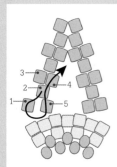

STEP 1
When you come to the end of the row of peyote stitch on the left-hand side of the petal, you will pick up the last B bead (bead 1) and have nowhere to anchor it. So to anchor bead 1, sew up through beads 5, 2, and 4 of the petal.

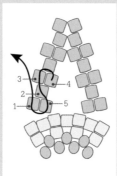

STEP 2
Then take the thread across and sew down through beads 3, 2, and 5. Finally, take the thread across and sew up though bead 1. You are now ready to add the next row of peyote stitch to the petal.

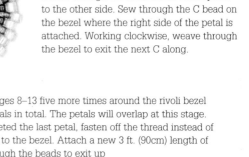

Bead KEY			
A	B	C	D

REVERSE SIDE

Stages 15–20 are worked with the reverse side facing.

STAGE 15 Stages 15–18 form the first duo bead petal. Working with the reverse side of the pendant facing you, pick up 1D, 1A, and 1D. Sew down through the B at the bottom corner of the next petal. Pick up 1D and sew up through the B at the corner of the original petal, the first D added in this stage, and the next B on the same petal.

STAGE 16 Pick up 1D and 1A. Sew through the empty hole of the A from stage 15. Pick up 1A and 1D. Sew down through 1B, 1D, and 1B of the next petal, through the D connecting to the original petal, and then up through the next 1B, 1D, 1B, and 1D of the original petal.

STAGE 17 Pick up 3D and sew through the empty hole of the next A. Pick up 1A and sew through the next A. Pick up 3D and sew down through the next D. Weave through the beads until you exit the first 3D added in this stage. You may need to use pliers to ease the needle through, but take care not to break the beads. If you find that you cannot pass through the D beads, weave through the B beads around them instead.

STAGE 18 Pick up 3D and sew through the empty hole of the top A. Pick up 5D and sew back through the A. Pick up 3D and sew down through the next 3D. Weave through the peyote petal until you exit the opposite bottom corner.

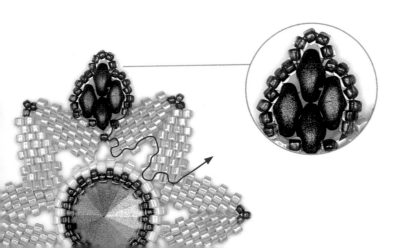

STAGE 19 Repeat stages 15–18 five more times to make six duo bead petals in total. After making the final duo bead petal, weave back through this petal until you exit the middle D bead at the top. To make the hanging loop, pick up 8D and sew back through the middle D on the petal and the first 2D just added.

STAGE 20 [Pick up 1D and sew through the next 2D] three times. Sew around all these beads again. This completes the hanging loop.

STAGE 21 Turn the pendant over so that the front is facing you. Weave through the beads toward the rivoli until you exit the indicated C bead from stage 7; the thread should exit this bead in a counterclockwise direction. Alternatively, fasten off and begin a new thread here.

Weave through to exit this C, ready to work counterclockwise around the rivoli bezel.

STAGE 22 *Pick up 1A and sew through the next C. Peyote stitch 2C around the bezel.** Repeat from * to ** five more times. Sew through the first A added in this stage and the next 2C.

STAGE 23 *Pick up 1C and sew through the next C from stage 22. Pick up 3D and sew through the empty hole of the next A. Pick up 3D and sew through the next C from stage 22.** Repeat from * to ** five more times. Weave in the remaining thread, fasten off securely, and trim. Fasten off any remaining tail threads. Add a bail to the loop with a jump ring, ready to hang from some ribbon, chain, or cord.

Stages 22–23 form the corona at the center of the flower pendant.

Iona Pendant

The gleaming crystal rivoli in this enchanting pendant is surrounded by two layers of duo beads and highlighted with pearls. You can make the pendant using contrasting colors, or shades of one color for equally striking effect. You can replace the pearls with crystal beads if you wish.

Finished diameter: 2 in. (5cm) excluding bail

YOU WILL NEED (beads shown actual size)

BEAD BOX
- **A** = 5g duo beads, turquoise

- **B** = 6g duo beads, green

- **C** = 2g 11º seed beads, green

- **D** = Eight 4mm glass pearls, aqua

- **F** = One 14mm crystal rivoli, green

HARDWARE
- 7 ft. (2.1m) thread
- Cord, ribbon, or chain with clasp

TOOLKIT
- Size 11 or 12 beading needle
- Scissors

Tip Adapting the size of bezel

For future projects that you might like to design yourself, here is a table showing how many C and D beads to pick up for the stage 1 circle for different sizes of rivoli. For larger rivolis, you may also be more comfortable adding an extra row of C beads to the bezel.

Rivoli	Stage 1 circle
12mm	[1C, 1D] six times
14mm	[1C, 1D] eight times
16mm	[1C, 1D] nine times
18mm	[1C, 1D] ten times

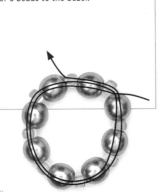

STAGE 1 Stages 1–5 form the netted bezel that holds the rivoli (see also technique panel below). Thread the needle with 3 ft. (90cm) of thread and pick up [1C, 1D] eight times. Sew through all the beads again in the same direction to form a circle, leaving a tail of thread to weave in later. Sew through the first C, D, and C again.

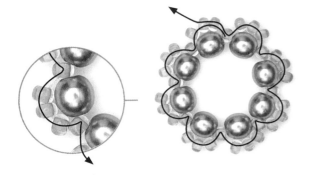

STAGE 2 *Pick up 3C, skip the next D, and sew through the next C.** Repeat from * to ** seven more times, and then sew through the first 2C added in this stage.

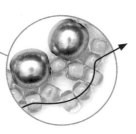

STAGE 3 *Pick up 3C and sew through the middle C of the next group of 3C from the previous stage.** Repeat from * to ** seven more times, and then sew through the first 2C added in this stage.

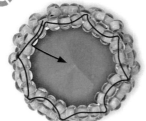

REVERSE SIDE

STAGE 4 Repeat stage 3 once more. The netting should begin to form a cup. Place the rivoli (F) face down into the netting, so that the front of the crystal is next to the pearls. Tighten the thread around it slightly, making sure it does not pop out again.

REVERSE SIDE

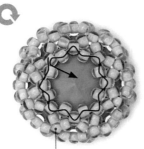

STAGE 5 *Pick up 1C and sew through the middle C of the next group of 3C from stage 4.** Repeat from * to ** seven more times. Pull the thread tight to cinch the beads together. Fasten off the thread and attach a new 4 ft. (1.2m) length to continue. Weave through the beads to exit the middle C of a group of 3C from stage 2.

At the end of stage 9, you will need to exit the middle C of a group of 3C from stage 3 (shown here for clarity).

At the end of stage 5, weave through to exit the middle C of a group of 3C from stage 2.

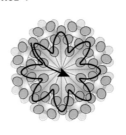

TECHNIQUE: DIAGRAM VIEW OF THE NETTED BEZEL

Note that the seed beads will gradually cup themselves toward you. After inserting the rivoli in stage 4, tighten the thread so that the seed beads cup around the crystal and hold it securely in place.

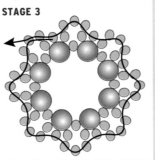

STAGE 2

STAGE 3

STAGE 4

STAGE 5

Exit bead

Bead KEY			
A	B	C	D

STAGE 6 *Pick up 3A and sew through the middle C of the next group of 3C from stage 2.** Repeat from * to ** seven more times. Sew through the first 3A added in this stage and then step up by sewing back through the empty hole of the A just exited.

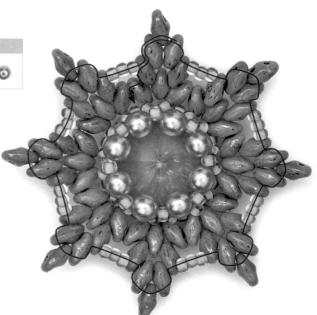

STAGE 7 *Pick up 1A and sew through the empty hole of the next A. Pick up 1A and sew through the next 2A.** Repeat from * to ** seven more times. Sew through the next 3A and then step up through the A just exited.

STAGE 9 *Pick up 1A and sew through the empty hole of the next A. Take the thread down between the beads and sew through the top hole of the next A. Sew through the next 3C and 1A. Take the thread up between the beads and sew through the top hole of the next A.** Repeat from * to ** seven more times. Weave through the beads until you exit the middle C of a group of 3C from stage 3 (see starting point of thread on photograph below, plus the photograph of the underside of the finished bezel shown with stage 5 on page 103, to help you locate the correct exit bead).

REVERSE SIDE

STAGE 8 *Pick up 2A and sew through the empty hole of the next A. Pick up 3C and sew through the next A.** Repeat from * to ** seven more times. Sew through the next 2A and then step up through the A just exited.

STAGE 10 Now work with the reverse side facing you. *Pick up 3B and sew through the middle C of the next 3C from stage 3.** Repeat from * to ** seven more times. Sew through the first 3B added in this stage and then step up through the B just exited.

REVERSE SIDE

STAGE 11 *Pick up 1B and sew through the next B. Pick up 1B and sew through the next 2B.** Repeat from * to ** seven more times. Sew through the next 3B and then step up through the B just exited.

REVERSE SIDE

STAGE 12 *Pick up 2B and sew through the next B. Pick up 3C and sew through the next B.** Repeat from * to ** seven more times. Sew through the first 2B added in this stage and then step up through the B just exited.

REVERSE SIDE

STAGE 13 *Pick up 1B and sew through the empty hole of the next B. Take the thread down between the beads and sew through the top hole of the next B. Sew through the next 3C and 1B. Take the thread up between the beads and sew through the top hole of the next B.** Repeat from * to ** seven more times. Weave through the beads until you exit the middle C of the first 3C added in this stage.

STAGE 14 You will now make a simple duo bead bail. Pick up [1C, 1B] twelve times and 1C.

REVERSE SIDE

STAGE 15 Sew back through the middle C on the pendant to form a loop. [Pick up 1C and sew through the empty hole of the next B on the loop] twelve times. Pick up 1C and sew through the middle C and the next C on the pendant.

STAGE 16 Sew once more around both sides of the loop and through all 3C at the top of the pendant to secure the bail. Weave the remaining thread through the beads, knotting 4–5 times in between as you go, and then trim. Weave in and fasten off the beginning tail in the same way.

Cascade Necklace and Ring

Duo beads in rich peacock colors are used to capture and link four medallions, all centered with sparkling crystal rivolis, to create an elegant asymmetric necklace that sits on the décolletage with grace and style. A duo bead loop added to a fifth medallion makes a matching ring to complete the ensemble—perfect for that special evening.

Finished size: necklace 17 in. (43cm) inside, 22 in. (56cm) outside, including clasp; ring size is adjustable (the ring is shown on page 111).

YOU WILL NEED
(beads shown actual size)

BEAD BOX
- **A** = 10g duo beads, blue
- **B** = 9g duo beads, green
- **C** = 15g 11° seed beads, green
- **D** = Forty 4mm glass pearls, gold
- **E** = Five 14mm crystal rivolis, blue/green

HARDWARE
- 30 ft. (9.1m) thread

TOOLKIT
- Size 11 or 12 beading needle
- Scissors
- Pliers

Necklace

STAGES 1–5 Stages 1–13 form the rivoli medallion. Thread the needle with 3 ft. (90cm) of thread. Start by making a netted bezel around one of the rivolis (E) using C and D beads. To do this, follow stages 1–5 on page 103, but finish by exiting the middle C of a group of 3C from stage 3 rather than stage 2.

REVERSE SIDE

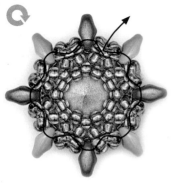

STAGE 6 You will now add a ring of duo beads around the lower side of the bezel, so work with the back of the bezel facing you. *Pick up 1C, 1A, and 1C. Sew through the middle C in the next group of 3C from stage 3. Pick up 1C, 1B, and 1C. Sew through the middle C of the next group of 3C from stage 3.** Repeat from * to ** three more times.

STAGE 7 Weave through the beads until you exit a C from the original stage 1 circle and turn the bezel over so that the front is facing you. You will now add a ring of duo beads around the upper side of the bezel, making sure that the duo bead colors in each position match those added in stage 6. *Pick up 1C, 1 duo bead in the correct color, and 1C. Sew through the next C in the stage 1 circle.** Repeat from * to ** seven more times. Sew through the first few beads added in this stage until you exit a B bead, and then step up by sewing back through the empty hole of the same B.

Make sure that the colors of the upper and lower duo beads match.

STAGE 8 You will now add groups of beads around the side of the bezel, joining together the duo beads from stages 6–7. Pick up 1B and 3C. Sew through the empty hole of the B just added and the B on the lower side of the bezel.

STAGE 9 Pick up 1B and 3C. Sew through the empty hole of the B just added and the B on the upper side of the bezel. Sew through the next 1B and 2C from stage 8. This completes the first group of side beads.

STAGE 10
To add the second group of side beads, pick up 1C and 1A. Sew through the A on the lower side of the bezel.

STAGE 11
Pick up 1A and 3C. Sew through the empty hole of the A just added, the upper A, and the A from stage 10. Pick up 1C and sew through the middle C from the first group of side beads (the C exited at the end of stage 9). Sew through the next 1C, 3A and 2C of this group of side beads.

STAGE 12 Repeat stages 8–11 twice more and then stages 8–9 once again to add groups of beads in alternating colors around the side of the bezel. For the final group, pick up 1C and 1A. Sew through the A on the lower side of the bezel. Pick up 1A and 1C. Sew through the middle C of the first group of side beads.

STAGE 13 Pick up 1C and sew through the empty hole of the second A added in this group, the upper A, and the first A added in this group. Pick up 1C and sew through the middle C of the adjacent group of side beads. Sew around this final group of side beads once more to tighten. Weave the remaining thread through the beads, knotting 4–5 times in between as you go, and then trim. Weave in and fasten off the beginning tail in the same way.

When making the fourth medallion (stage 14), you will sew around to exit the lower hole of this A bead, working inward, instead of fastening off.

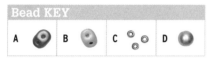

Bead KEY

A   B   C   D

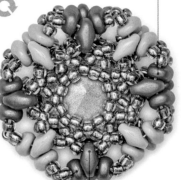

REVERSE SIDE

At the end of stage 14, exit this A, working toward the other A beads.

STAGE 14 Repeat stages 1–13 to make four medallions in total, but make the fourth one using 4 ft. (1.2m) of thread and do not fasten off at the end. Instead, continue sewing through the last group of side beads until you exit the lower hole of the A bead indicated, working inward.

You will need to exit an outer A, working away from the other A beads, for stage 31.

To make the ring, exit the underside hole of a middle A.

REVERSE SIDE

Work stage 15 onward with the reverse side facing.

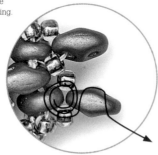

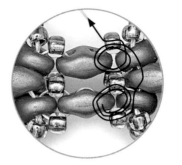

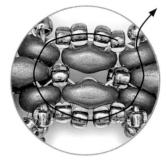

STAGE 15 You will now link two medallions together, working with the back of the medallions facing you. Pick up 1C, 1A, and 1C. Sew through the lower A again and then through all four beads once more to tighten. Sew through the next 2A in the medallion.

STAGE 16 Pick up 1C, 1A, and 1C, and sew through the A just exited. Sew through all the beads again to tighten, and finish by stepping up by sewing through the empty hole of the A just added.

STAGE 17 Pick up 1C and sew through the lower A on the next medallion, to match the first. Pick up 1C and sew through the A from stage 16. Sew through all four beads again to tighten. Sew through the first C added in this stage and 3A on the second medallion. Pick up 1C and sew through the A from stage 15. Pick up 1C and sew through the last A on the medallion. Sew through all four beads again and then through the outer C once more.

STAGE 18 Pick up 2C and sew through the next outer C, lower 3A, and outer C on the first medallion. Pick up 2C and sew through the next outer C and lower 3A on the second medallion. Weave around the second medallion until you exit the lower A of the group of side beads on the opposite side.

Repeat stages 15–16 to form the first links in the neck strap.

STAGE 19 Repeat stages 15–18 to join the third medallion. Finish by exiting the lower A on the opposite side as before. You will now start forming the wide section of the neck strap. Add a new 4 ft. (1.2m) length of thread at this point. Repeat stages 15–16 to form the first duo bead links in the strap.

STAGE 20 Pick up 4C, 1B, and 4C. Sew through the A just exited and then the first 4C and 1B again. Step up through the B.

STAGE 21 Pick up 4C, 1B, and 4C. Sew through the B just exited and then the first 4C and 1B again. Step up through the B. Pick up 4C, 1A, and 4C. Sew through the B just exited and then the first 4C and 1A again. Step up through the A.

STAGE 22 Repeat stages 20–21 six more times, but do not step up through the final A. Instead, sew through 3C of the last group of 4C added, so that you are now working back toward the medallions.

STAGE 23 Pick up 1C, 1B, 4C, 1A, and 1C. Sew through the middle 2C of the adjacent link on the first side of the neck strap. Sew around these beads once more to tighten, and finish by exiting the B just added. Step up through the same B.

STAGE 24 Pick up 1C and sew through the middle 2C of the adjacent link on the first side of the neck strap. Pick up 1C, 1B, and 4C and sew back through the previous B of this link. Sew through the next 1C of this link, the middle 2C on the adjacent link, and the next 1C and 1B of this link. Step up through the same B. Pick up 1C and sew through the middle 2C of the next adjacent link. Pick up 1C, 1A, and 4C and sew back through the previous B of this link. Sew through the next 1C of this link, the middle 2C on the adjacent link, and the next 1C and 1A of this link. Step up through the same A.

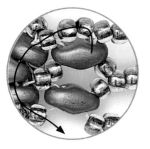

STAGE 25 Repeat stages 23–24 six more times but do not step up through the last A. Instead, pick up 2C and sew through the next outer C, lower 3A, and outer C on the medallion.

STAGE 26 *Pick up 2C and sew through the next 4C along the bottom of the neck strap.** Repeat from * to ** all along this side of the strap, until you exit the last 4C.

STAGE 27 Pick up 2C and sew through the empty hole of the next A. Pick up 1A and sew through the next A.

STAGE 28 Pick up 3C and sew through the empty hole of the last A added. Pick up 3C and sew back through the adjoining holes of the 3A. Sew through the first 3C just added and the last A. Pick up 5C and sew through the last A again. Sew back through the first 3C just added, so that you exit the middle C at the end of the strap.

Sew around the loop four times.

STAGE 29 Pick up 4C and sew through the attachment ring on one half of the clasp. Pick up 3C and sew down through the first of the 4C and then through the middle C at the end of the neck strap. Sew around this loop of beads three more times for strength.

STAGE 30 Weave through the next 5C along the top of the neck strap and then repeat stage 26. Weave in and fasten off the remaining thread and any tail ends. Orientate this section of the necklace as shown on page 110, with the reverse side facing you.

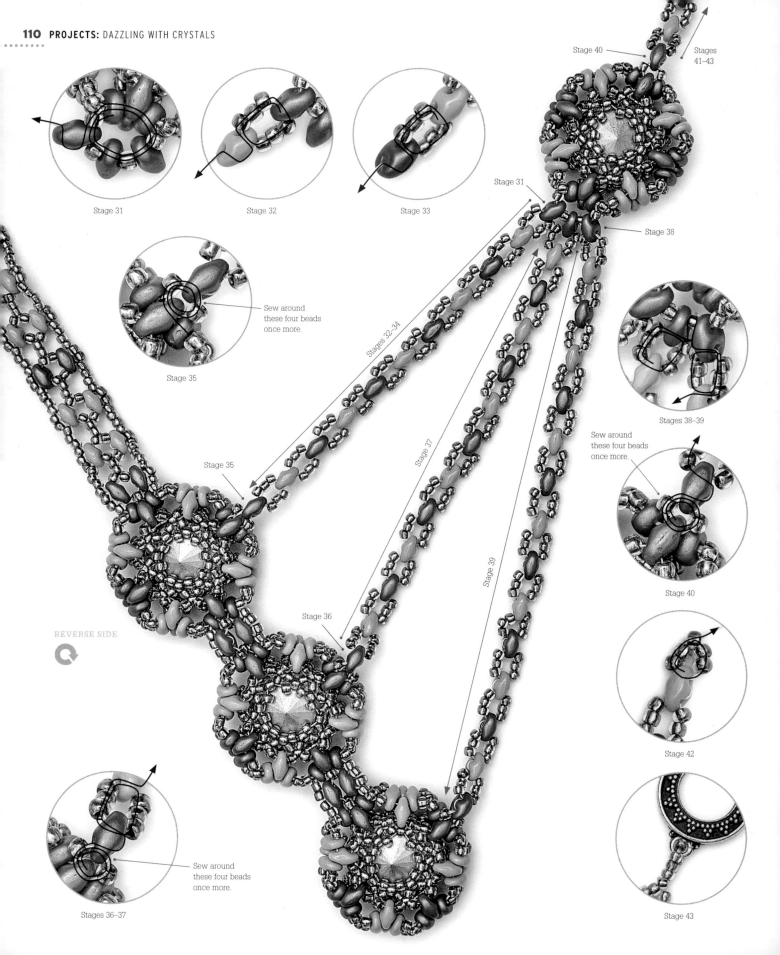

Stage 31

Stage 32

Stage 33

Stage 31

Stage 40

Stages 41–43

Stage 38

Sew around these four beads once more.

Stage 35

Stages 38–39

Stages 32–34

Stage 35

Stage 37

Stage 39

Sew around these four beads once more.

Stage 40

Stage 36

REVERSE SIDE

Stage 42

Sew around these four beads once more.

Stages 36–37

Stage 43

CASCADE NECKLACE AND RING **111**

Bead KEY

A ● B ● C ○○○ D ●

STAGE 31 Attach a 2 ft. (60cm) thread to the remaining single medallion, weaving through the beads to exit a lower A on the side, working away from the group of A beads (see stage 14). Pick up [1C, 1A] three times and 1C. Sew through the 3A on the medallion and then through all of the beads once more, exiting the first A just added. Step up through the same A.

STAGE 32 Pick up 3C, 1B, and 3C. Sew back through the A and the first 3C and 1B just added. Step up through the same B.

STAGE 33 Pick up 3C, 1A, and 3C. Sew back through the B and the first 3C and 1A just added. Step up through the same A.

STAGE 34 Repeat stages 32–33 four more times.

STAGE 35 Pick up 1C and sew through the middle lower A of the group of A on the top medallion on the wide strap. Pick up 1C and sew through the last A on the narrow strap. Sew around these beads twice more for strength, then fasten off.

STAGE 36 Attach a 3 ft. (90cm) thread to the middle medallion on the wide strap, weaving through the beads to exit the lower middle A of the side group. Pick up 1C, 1A, and 1C. Sew back through the A on the medallion. Sew through all four beads twice more for strength, exiting the A just added. Step up through this A.

STAGE 37 Repeat stages 32–33 five times, then stage 32 again.

STAGE 38 Pick up 3C and sew through the middle A added to the single medallion in stage 31. Pick up 3C and sew back through the B on the strap, the first 3C just added, and the A on the medallion again. Weave through the medallion to exit the empty hole of the third A added in stage 31.

STAGE 39 Repeat stages 32–33 seven times. Repeat stage 35 to join the narrow strap to the bottom medallion on the wide strap.

STAGE 40 Attach a 3 ft. (90cm) thread to the single medallion and weave through the beads to exit the lower middle A opposite those you have just been working on. Pick up 1C, 1A, and 1C. Sew back through the A on the medallion. Sew through all four beads twice more for strength, exiting the A just added. Step up through this A.

STAGE 41 Repeat stages 32–33 six times, then stage 32 again.

STAGE 42 Pick up 5C and sew through the last B on the strap to make a small loop. Sew through the first 3C again.

STAGE 43 Repeat stage 29 to attach the other half of the clasp. Weave in and fasten off the thread.

Ring

See it GROW

STAGES 1–13 Using 5 ft. (1.5m) of thread, follow stages 1–13 on page 107 to make a single medallion. Finish by exiting the hole of a middle A on the underside of the medallion (see stage 14 of the necklace on page 108).

STAGE 14 Pick up 2C and 1A. Sew through the empty hole of the same A. Pick up 2C and sew back through the middle A on the medallion. Sew around these beads once more to tighten, exiting the first hole of the A just added.

STAGE 15 Pick up [1C, 1A] eleven times. This will give you a size US 7 ring (UK O; EU 55¼). You can adjust this number as required for a larger or smaller ring. Pick up an extra 1C and 1A for one size larger; pick up 1C and 1A fewer for one size smaller.

STAGE 16 Pick up 2C and sew through the underside hole of the middle A on the opposite side of the medallion. Pick up 2C and sew through the empty hole of the next A on the ring band. Sew around these beads once more, exiting the second hole of the A just added.

STAGE 17 *Pick up 1C and sew through the next A.** Repeat from * to ** all along this side of the ring band. Sew around both sides of the band several times to stiffen it a little. Weave in and fasten off the thread.

Index

A
Alicia Bracelet 74-77
awl 15, 18

B
bails 14, 20-21, 97, 105
bangles see bracelets
Beach Mai Bracelet 36-37
bead mat 15, 16
bead scoop 15
beaded findings:
    bails 20-21, 97, 105
    toggle clasps 22-23
beads:
    organizing 16
    types 12-13
    unblocking holes 18
bezels 95, 103
bracelets:
    Alicia 74-77
    Beach Mai 36-37
    Cascara 60-63
    Crystal Bloom 91-93
    Daisy Chain 52-54
    Daisy Mai 40-41
    Demi Tuile 50-51
    Diamond Twist 64-67
    Petits Secrets 69-71
    Tic Tac Mai 38-39
    Trinity 31-33

C
Cascade Necklace and Ring
    22-23, 106-111
Cascara Bangle 24, 60-63
chains 14
clasps 14
    attaching 19
color:
    contrast 26
    designing with 24-27
    inspiration 27
    palettes 27
    theory 24
    wheel 24
complementary colors 24, 25
cord 14
Corona Pendant 98-101
crystal beads 13
Crystal Bloom Bracelet 91-93
cull rates 12
cylinder beads 13

D
Daisy Chain Bracelet 26, 52-54
Daisy Mai Bracelet 40-41
Demi Tuile Bracelet 50-51
Diamond Twist Bracelet 26,
    64-67
double overhand knot 17
drop beads 13
duo beads 12, 13

E
ear wires/hooks 14
earrings:
    Honesty 72-73
    Santi Drop 58-59

F
findings 14
    beaded 20-23, 97, 105

H
half-hitch knot 17
hardware 14
harmonious colors 24, 25
Honesty Earrings 72-73

I
Iona Pendant 20, 102-105

J
jump rings 14
    attaching clasp with 19
    opening and closing 19

K
knots 17

L
lighting 27

M
Mai Tile 34-35
    Bracelet Trio 34-41
Mimosa Necklace 25, 55-57
mistakes, fixing 12

N
necklaces:
    Cascade 106-110
    New Leaf 47-49
    Mimosa 55-57
    Savannah 86-89
    Sparkling Swags 82-85
    Summer Stars 42-45
    Wisteria 78-81
    see also pendants
needles 15

netted bezel 103
neutral colors 24, 25
New Leaf Necklace 25, 47-49

O
overhand knot 17

P
pearls 13
pendant fittings 14, 20
pendants:
    Corona 98-101
    Iona 102-105
    Triskele 94-97
Petits Secrets Bracelet 69-71
peyote stitch bezel 95
pliers 12, 15, 19

R
ribbon 14
ring: Cascade 106, 111
rivolis 13

S
Santi Drop Earrings 25, 58-59
Savannah Necklace 26-27,
    86-89
scissors 15
seed beads 12
shades 24, 25
Sparkling Swags Necklace
    82-85
square knot 17
stepping up 18-19
stop bead 18
Summer Stars Necklace
    42-45
SuperDuos 12, 13

T
techniques, basic 16-19
thread:
    attaching/fastening off 17
    length 17
    types 14
Tic Tac Mai Bracelet 38-39
tints 24, 25
tonal value/contrast 26
toolkit 15
Trinity Bracelet 13, 31-33
Triskele Pendant 24, 94-97
turn bead 18-19
Twin beads 12, 13
two-hole beads 12, 13

W
Wisteria Necklace 78-81

Credits

Author's acknowledgments
• For Chris, my long-suffering partner, thanks for all the support, belief, and cooking, enabling me to keep on beading without making you wait for dinner.
• Also for Didy, my beady friend, who helped give me a good start in becoming a bead designer and pattern writer.
• For all the beading ladies and gentlemen who have shown me the way through your books and articles over the years. Without you, I wouldn't have a clue.
• Lastly, to Robin's Beads, my number one supplier, who has patiently supplied my beads and never let me down: **www.robins-beads.co.uk**

Picture credits
page 24: The color wheel is based on the Rainbow Color Selector, courtesy of K1C2, LLC. page 27: Flower images courtesy of www.shutterstock.com: fotohunter (left); ZoranKrstic (center); ra3rn (right).

All other photographs and illustrations are the copyright of Quarto Publishing plc. While every effort has been made to credit contributors, Quarto would like to apologize should there have been any omissions or errors—and would be pleased to make the appropriate correction for future editions of the book.